THE
NUTRiBULLET
RECIPE BOOK

LEGAL DISCLAIMER

It's a fact: readers who follow an ACTION GUIDE as they read and use cookbooks tend to have the most success!

Here's what I'm going to do to thank you for downloading my book. Go to the link below to instantly sign up for these bonuses.

Here's just a taste of what subscribers get:

Printable Kitchen Guides:

- Keep your food fresher for longer with the Extra-Long Food Storage Guide
- No more guess work in the kitchen -- Metric Conversion Guide
- Make delicious spreads in minutes -- Easy Spreads Guide
- Protect your family from consuming undercooked meat -- Meat Grilling Guide
- Many more new upcoming high-quality guides

Books and Recipes:

- New mouth-watering recipes you have NEVER tried before
- New books I publish for FREE

GRAB YOUR FREEBIES NOW AT
COOKINGWITHAFOODIE.COM

Contents

Blender Showroom 1
   High-End Blenders 1
   Standard Blenders 2

Drink Smoothies to Feel Incredible & Look Sexy 3

Juicing vs Blending: What's The Difference? 5

Tips & Techniques 6
   How To Save 10+ Hours A Week 6
   Superfood Guide 9

Nutribullet Blender Tips 11
   Easy Cleaning Tips 12
   Some Great Tricks 12

Recipes 16
  I. 100 Smoothie recipes
    A. 20 Superfood Recipes
     1. Blueberry flax superfood smoothie 17
     2. Superfood power smoothie 17
     3. Mint chip superfood smoothie 18
     4. Maca almond cacao smoothie 18
     5. Vegan superfood chocolate smoothie 18
     6. Avocado superfood smoothie 18
     7. Green coconut smoothie (healthy) 18
     8. Banana beet smoothie 18
     9. Green smoothie 19
    10. Berry blast almond smoothie 19
    11. Blueberry mango and superfood smoothie 19
    12. Superfood pb banana and cacao green smoothie 19
    13. Superfood pumpkin pie smoothie 19
    14. Superfood chia green smoothie 20

15. Chocolate-cauliflower smoothie recipes from 'superfood smoothies' 20
16. Superfood triple berry chia pudding................. 20
17. Chocolate malt superfood smoothie.................. 20
18. Eggless nog superfood smoothie..................... 20
19. Spicy citrus and berry smoothie with chia seeds....... 21
20. Blueberry avocado and spinach superfood smoothie.... 21

B. 20 High-protein recipes
21. Banana raspberry chia smoothie..................... 21
22. Strawberry banana smoothie with chia seeds 21
23. Blueberry mango smoothie 22
24. Papaya ginger smoothie 22
25. Peanut butter and jelly protein smoothie............. 22
26. French toast protein shake 22
27. Chocolate peanut butter protein smoothie............ 22
28. Green warrior protein smoothie 23
29. Coconut almond protein shake 23
30. Blueberry pineapple oatmeal smoothie 23
31. Dark chocolate peppermint protein shake............ 23
32. Cherry almond smoothie 24
33. Chocolate espresso protein smoothie 24
34. Roasted strawberry protein smoothie................ 24
35. Green vanilla almond post-workout shake 24
36. Strawberry almond protein dream smoothie.......... 24
37. Orange mango recovery smoothie 25
38. The peanut butter power protein shake 25
39. Winter mint chocolate protein shake 25
40. Cherry ginger lime smoothie 25

C. 20 Weight-loss recipes
41. Fat burning green tea and vegetable smoothie 26
42. Crisp apple smoothie.............................. 26
43. 4 Ingredient green smoothie 26
44. 5 Ingredient creamy banana green smoothie.......... 26
45. Green superfood smoothie......................... 26

46. Tropical greens smoothie 26
47. Blueberry pineapple green detox smoothie 27
48. Raspberry mango chia seed smoothie 27
49. Tropical green smoothie 27
50. Rainbow smoothie 27
51. Fruity green smoothie. 28
52. Very cherry green smoothie. 28
53. Creamy avocado kale smoothie 28
54. Berries and oats smoothie. 28
55. Green blueberry banana smoothie 28
56. Lulu's green smoothie 29
57. Blueberry peach kale chia smoothie 29
58. Green smoothie bowl 29
59. Grape mango kale smoothie. 29
60. Green goodness in a glass 29
D. 10 Anti-aging recipes
61. Blueberry peach anti aging smoothie 30
62. Anti-aging turmeric smoothie. 30
63. Chocolate berry almond blast 30
64. Blueberry detox smoothie. 30
65. Alkaline cleansing smoothie. 30
66. Tangerine turmeric antioxidant smoothie 31
67. Red grape, plum, and raspberry antioxidant smoothie . . 31
68. An anti-aging smoothie 31
69. Go, go, goji blast. 31
70. Watermelon smoothie. 31
E. 10 Detoxification recipes
71. Detox smoothie 32
72. Detox blueberry fruit smoothie. 32
73. Citrus & green tea detox smoothie 32
74. Lemon ginger detox drink 32
75. Detox beet and carrot smoothie. 32
76. Grapefruit-cado sunrise smoothie. 32
77. Natural daily detox remedy drink 33

78. Matcha mango pineapple smoothie 33
79. Spring cleaning detox 33
80. Cranberry bliss detox smoothie. 33

F. 10 Energy boosting recipes
81. Afternoon energy smoothie 33
82. Energy boost fruit smoothie. 34
83. Blueberry almond butter smoothies 34
84. Fruit and veggie smoothie 34
85. Mango-strawberry watermelon smoothie 34
86. Raw mango lassi love. 34
87. Dr. Oz's energy boost smoothie 34
88. Lush cherry and coconut smoothie. 35
89. Kiwi & green tea smoothie 35
90. Peanut butter and banana oatmeal smoothie. 35

G. 10 High-calorie recipes (to stay full longer)
91. Strawberry mango and almond smoothie 35
92. Raspberry cheesecake smoothie 35
93. Sweet potato and banana pie smoothie. 36
94. Tropical protein shake smoothie 36
95. Morning energy blast 36
96. Almond butter me up!. 36
97. Energy blast citrus green smoothie. 36
98. Pineapple ginger energy blast. 36
99. Almond delight 37
100. Chocolate-covered cherry smoothie. 37

II. 100 Juice recipes
1. Carrot, pear, raspberry, cucumber juice 38
2. Pinky promise me carrot juice 38
3. Beet green, carrot, apple, orange juice. 39
4. The ultimate green power juice 39
5. Lauren's favorite green juice 39
6. V8 juice 39
7. Grapefruit veggie lime juice 39
8. Grapefruit mint juice. 39
9. Carrot, orange, and ginger juice without juicer 40

10. Green juice without a juicer 40
11. Watermelon raspberry lime juice 40
12. Beet happy juice 40
13. Watermelon juice 40
14. Green juice in a blender 40
15. Fresh strawberry juice with coconut water 41
16. Purple rain detox juice 41
17. Ginger cucumber detox juice 41
18. Pina colada pineapple detox juice 41
19. Holly's green juice 41
20. Pear and carrot detox juice 41
21. Green juice 41
22. Ginger beet juice 42
23. Kale grape ginger lemon juice 42
24. Peachy keen 42
25. Fennel & apple detox green juice 42
26. Orange cream juice 42
27. Ricki heller's cranberry, pomegranate holiday detox juice .. 42
28. Carrot ginger juice 42
29. Broccoli juice 43
30. Classic beet juice 43
31. Plum and ginger detox juice 43
32. Green juice for beginners 43
33. Lean & mean green juice 43
34. Primavera green juice 43
35. Popeye potion 43
36. Pineapple green juice 43
37. Green goddess juice 44
38. Beet coconut juice and juicing without a juicer 44
39. Green juice ii 44
40. Sweet freedom's green juice 44
41. Feel better green juice 44
42. Stay healthy green juice 44
43. Hippie juice 45
44. Carrot apple glow juice 45

45. Beet & berry liver cleanse juice 45
46. Grapefruit strawberry juice 45
47. Beet carrot lemon apple kale celery ginger juice 45
48. Pineapple ginger paradise 45
49. Beetroot juice 46
50. Busy bee detox juice 46
51. Midnight juice 46
52. Everyday detox juice 46
53. Green detox juice 46
54. Liver detox juice 46
55. Blood orange chili juice 46
56. Pineapple detox juice 46
57. Spinach shots 47
58. Red reviver 47
59. Orange broccoli juice 47
60. Green gunslinger 47
61. Rhubarb juice 47
62. Cranberry pomegranate and kale juice 47
63. Spiced apple cider juice 47
64. Tomato with a kick 47
65. Energizer bunny on crack juice 48
66. Sweet curb appetite juice 48
67. Green gut begone! 48
68. Beet blood infusion juice 48
69. Strong core juice 48
70. Mean green juice 48
71. Bright-eyed green juice 48
72. Iron and vitamin c boosting green juice 49
73. Skin rejuvenating green juice 49
74. Lean green power juice 49
75. Fat dissolver juice 49
76. Healthy colada green juice recipe 49
77. Think green juice 49
78. Bluepeary juice 50

79. Magenta zing 50
80. Dark knight. 50
81. Leftovers 50
82. Citrus sensation 50
83. Bright green goodness. 50
84. Delicious mint refresher 50
85. Mango tango. 50
86. Green and orange power. 51
87. Red carrot envy 51
88. Kale surprise. 51
89. Miracle cure juice. 51
90. Light and lemony aloe juice 51
91. Health aloe juice. 51
92. Exotic aloe vera juice. 51
93. Fresh & fruity jungle juice 52
94. No more sinus 52
95. Cancer fighting green juice. 52
96. Orange, spinach and mint 52
97. Liver cleanse grape juice 52
98. Liver detoxification vegetable juice 52
99. Belly buster green juice. 53
100. Reboot essentials 53

III. 25 Nut milk recipes

1. Plain almond milk 54
2. Cashew milk 54
3. Easy homemade horchata. 54
4. Cashew milk lattes 54
5. Raw cacao hazelnut milk. 55
6. Vanilla cinnamon almond milk 55
7. Turmeric almond milk 55
8. Nut milk with chocolate hazelnut and
   honey cinnamon cashew. 55
9. Homemade raw vegan brazil nut milk 55
10. Pistachio milk. 56

11. Homemade pecan milk. 56
12. Strawberry macadamia nut milk 56
13. Cashew cream. 56
14. Green cashew nut milk 56
15. Vanilla bean cashew milk 56
16. Homemade macadamia nut milk 56
17. Decadent almond macadamia milk 57
18. Homemade almond macadamia iced coffee 57
19. Walnut coconut milk with turmeric and cinnamon 57
20. Banana almond and oat smoothie - zupas 57
21. Pumpkin spice almond milk 57
22. Vanilla walnut milk 58
23. Chestnut praline latte 58
24. Iced almond-macadamia milk latte. 58
25. Orange splash pistachio milk. 58

IV. 10 Nut butter recipes

1. Homemade almond butter 59
2. Pecan butter 59
3. Walnut butter 60
4. Chocolate hazelnut butter spread 60
5. Cashew butter. 60
6. Pistachio butter. 60
7. Pine nut butter 60
8. Macadamia nut butter. 60
9. Brazil nut butter 60
10. Homemade vanilla cashew butter 60

V. 25 Easy soup recipes

1. Minestrone soup 62
2. Turkey meatball spinach tortellini soup 62
3. Hearty vegetable soup 63
4. Creamy potato soup. 63
5. Copycat panera creamy tomato basil soup. 63
6. 5 - Ingredient broccoli cheese soup. 63
7. 8 Can taco soup 64

8. Roasted cauliflower and broccoli white cheddar soup . . . 64
9. Sausage, potato and spinach soup 64
10. Best ever mushroom soup 64
11. Quick and easy tomato soup 65
12. Creamy chicken and mushroom soup 65
13. Easy chicken and rice soup. 65
14. Quick & easy chinese noodle soup 66
15. Olive garden's homemade zuppa toscana soup 66
16. Easy cheeseburger soup. 66
17. Miso soup 66
18. Best butternut squash soup. 67
19. Mexican lime soup w/ chicken. 67
20. Creamy sweet potato soup 67
21. Easy chicken noodle soup. 67
22. Chicken enchilada soup 68
23. Roasted red pepper soup. 68
24. 5-Ingredient easy white chicken chili 68
25. Chicken quinoa soup. 68

VI. 25 Fresh spice blends
1. Barbecue circuit rub 69
2. Cajun spice mix 69
3. Chili and taco seasoning. 69
4. Creole seasoning blend 70
5. Greek seasoning 70
6. Greek seasoning for chicken gyros 70
7. Montreal steak seasoning 70
8. Old bay seasoning 70
9. Pickling spice recipe 71
10. Steak fajita spice blend. 71
11. Poultry seasoning. 71
12. Spicy sweet potato fries spice mix 71
13. Taco seasoning 71
14. Zippy lemon pepper rub. 72
15. Basic curry powder 72

16. Chinese 5 spice blend 72
17. Egyptian dukkah 72
18. Adobo seasoning 72
19. Garam masala. 72
20. Ethiopian berbere. 73
21. Apple pie spice blend. 73
22. Chai spice blend. 73
23. Gingerbread spice mix. 73
24. Yellow curry powder 73
25. Za'atar seasoning blend 73

VII. 25 Flavored coffee & tea blends

1. Skinny vanilla frappuccino. 74
2. Chai tea fauxccino 74
3. Peppermint mocha frappe 74
4. Strawberry lemonade herbal tea 74
5. Youthberry wild orange blossom tea blend 75
6. Chocolate chip cookie coffee creamer. 75
7. Skinny ice blended mocha 75
8. Chocolate fudge sundae iced coffee. 75
9. Green tea frappe. 75
10. Lavender tea 76
11. Jack frost tea 76
12. Make your own tranquil tea blend. 76
13. Nettle cinnamon herbal tea infusion. 76
14. After-dinner digestive tea 76
15. Apple green tea turmeric tonic. 76
16. Homemade black apple tea mix. 76
17. Rosy black tea. 77
18. Russian tea (no powdered mix) 77
19. Schisandra five-flavored tea 77
20. Vitamin c herbal infusion. 77
21. Skinny mint chocolate chip frappucino 77
22. Coconut water iced coffee. 78
23. French vanilla coffee creamer. 78

24. Lemon balm tea 78
25. Homemade cinnamon coffee 78

VIII. 20 Milkshake recipes

1. Cake batter milkshake 79
2. Frozen caramel hot chocolate 79
3. Cookie monster ice cream 79
4. Strawberry nutella milkshake 79
5. Kit kat milkshake 80
6. Mini s'more brownie 80
7. Nerds milkshake 80
8. Super easy nutella milkshake 80
9. Strawberry milkshake 80
10. Cotton candy milkshake 80
11. Banana cream pie milkshake 80
12. Snickers & pretzel milkshake 81
13. Mocha mint milkshake 81
14. Red velvet milkshake 81
15. Toasted marshmallow milkshake 81
16. Coffee milkshake 81
17. Mango milkshake 81
18. Mint chip milkshake cupcakes 82
19. Chocolate cookie dough milkshake 82
20. Ultimate ice cream sundae milk 82

IX. 25 Diy whipped natural butters for hair, skin, and body

1. Whipped gingerbread body butter 83
2. Skin perfecting body butter 83
3. Homemade body butter with shea and coconut oil 83
4. Dreamy homemade lemon cream body butter 83
5. Mango body butter 83
6. Homemade body butter base 84
7. Whipped mocha body frosting 84
8. Cranberry body butter 84
9. Honey coconut body butter 84
10. Eczema relief body cream 84

11. Whipped shea butter for hair & body 84

12. Basic body butter 85

13. Cooling aloe and mint body lotion 85

14. Peppermint body butter 85

15. Homemade baby skin cream 85

16. Chocolate hazelnut body lotion 85

17. Whipped white chocolate body butter 85

18. Double chocolate body butter 85

19. Homemade nourishing face cream 86

20. Homemade face lotion 86

21. Whipped peppermint bark body butter 86

22. Pretty in pink body butter. 86

23. Beach butter balm 86

24. Lemon cream body butter. 86

25. Ultra healing foot cream 86

Blender Showroom

This section will do a quick breakdown of our overall impression of some of the most popular blenders on the market. We take into account the quality of the motor & blade, ease of use, and overall quality of food that is produced by each machine.

Some people use blenders only for smoothies and others for crushing ice and making simple liquids and spreads. More advanced cooks use them to mill grains, making hot soups and purees, even kneading dough and making batter.

High-End Blenders

Vitamix:

If you can shell out for the hefty $650 price tag, the Vitamix blender takes home the gold trophy. It is one seriously high-powered blender that can do it all -- there is literally no limit to what you can do with this machine.

Pros:
- blends just about anything
- grind nuts and seeds -- completely breaking apart cell walls, turning them to dust
- smash frozen fruit into a soft cream
- warm up soups, sauces and dips by spinning them at a whopping 240 mph

Cons:
- giant price tag

Side note: You can purchase a "factory reconditioned" machine for around $299 at their website. You basically get a refurbished model that is certified to work like a brand new one for nearly half the price! (Or google "Vitamix factory reconditioned")

Blendtec

A worthy rival to the Vitamix, it is also slightly more cost-effective than the Vitamix. Surprisingly, its actually a little more powerful with its 1560 watt machine (compared to Vitamix's 1380 watts).

Pros:
- easy to clean and get out food that is trapped under the blades.
- super powerful motor
- warms up pretty much any liquid

Cons:
- does not come with a tamper -- a tool used to push food into the blades
- cannot fill the pitcher all the way to the top and expect perfect blending
- can be louder than the Vitamix when blending

Standard Blenders

Nutribullet

A more recent contender in the high-speed blender market, it has quickly risen to fame for what it can do with its cheaper price tag (you can get one for $90-130). This machine comes at 600 watts, which is half the power of the Vitamix or Blendtec.

Pros:
- great price tag for what you get
- can grind nuts, grains and seeds
- can make most things as its opponents, but you just have to be more patient

Cons:
- the pitcher is only 24oz, so expect to make smaller quantities at a time
- its shelf life is questionable at best

Ninja Blender

Another popular contender in the blender market, this one tends to be more affordable. It comes with multiple blades, unlike any of the others we featured in our showroom, and eliminates the need for a tamper. It's spectacular design even features blades in the middle and top -- which is hard to find anywhere else.

This one is comparable to the Nutribullet, thus, if you are patient, you can achieve a lot with this blender for the price. That means you should expect to reblend certain recipes a few times to achieve great results.

Pros:
- much more affordable blender
- can make decent liquid foods
- great for making smoothies
- great for large amounts of liquids
- suitable for households with multiple people

Cons:
- not the strongest blender

Drink Smoothies to Feel Incredible & Look Sexy

1. **Easily consume fruits and vegetables.** Most people struggle to get their daily recommended dose of nutrients, so they resort to artificial methods such as pills and gummies. Smoothies are a fantastic way to nourish your body the most natural way possible -- fresh fruits and vegetables.
2. **So easy to make.** With a decent blender, you can quickly and effortlessly throw in fresh ingredients, blend, and be out the kitchen in under 5 minutes. So no excuses even for the busiest people.
3. **Easy weight loss.** Drop the extra weight without any extra effort by feeding your body the essential nutrients it needs, while satisfying your craving for sweet or savory foods. By using naturally sweet ingredients like honey, you can easily cut out the heavily-processed sugars that are so hard to avoid when eating out nowadays.
4. **Supercharge your energy and reduce cravings.** Because smoothies are basically pure nutrition (barring any sweeteners you add), you will

feel a surge of energy when you consistently feed your body natural fuel. This depends from person to person how long it takes to feel this way since some people's bodies need to readjust from processing garbage to natural foods. If you keep up these positive habits, your body will certainly reverse those old bad ones and start appreciating you for eating only high quality food. The best part is that you will also be less hungry often since you are satiating the internal systems with way fewer calories.

5. **Superior digestion and nutrient absorption.** Imagine how much chewing you would have to get through to swallow a plate of veggies and fruits. Let the blender do the work for you and easily gulp down all the natural fiber-y goodness to jumpstart your digestive processes. It takes a lot of effort to efficiently break down the foods you normally chew and swallow. You are actually allowing your body to more effectively absorb the nutrients you just fed it.

6. **Easy way to detox.** We bombard our bodies with countless artificial chemicals on a daily basis. These chemicals are called "free-radicals" and basically travel freely through your body, sometimes attaching to other chemicals to create new dangerous compounds (this is one way certain cancers form). Now you can easily introduce wonderful antioxidants that clear out these terrible toxins.

7. **Infinite options for flavor.** Because there are so many fruits, vegetables, spices and herbs, supplements, oils and fats, there is literally no limit to how many types of smoothies you can create. Seriously, how amazing is that? If you can't stand drinking the same thing everyday, this is a great way for you to mix up your meal plans. You will get excited about trying new things

8. **Feel sexy with gorgeous skin, hair and nails.** The influx of vitamins and minerals in your diet will have noticeable effects on the outside of your body also, not just your internal organ systems. If you drink smoothies regularly, you can expect your skin, hair and nails to glow radiantly and catch the attention of everyone around you.

9. **Stop getting sick.** You are equipping your body's natural defenses with an entire army of vitamins and minerals to literally destroy foreign substances that cause sickness.

10. **Overall happiness.** This one is the most endearing benefit you will experience. Because your body's overall functions -- that means everything from the inside to outside -- are working at their optimal levels, you will feel much more calm and happy for no "specific" reason.

Juicing vs Blending: What's The Difference?

While the answer to this question might be obvious to some, most people don't understand that there is, in fact, a clear difference between juicing and blending.

The easiest way to clear the confusion is to focus on one major quality in taste and consistency that differs between juices and smoothies. When juicing, the machine is extracting the water and the majority of the nutrients the produce contains -- but leaves the pulp behind. Blenders, on the other hand, smash every juicy bit and piece of the produce to create a thicker and fuller consistency (keeping the insoluble fiber that is also good for you).

This leaves only one more question on the table. Which is better for you?

The answer to this question will depend on your health goals. While both are great choices, just keep a few things in mind:

- Because juice retains only soluble fiber, nutrients pass through your system much more quickly (easy digestion)
- Smoothies will keep you full longer since digesting them takes a little longer
- You can easily consume more produce when juicing (but that means no thick fruits like bananas or avocados)

Tips & Techniques

How To Save 10+ Hours A Week

So you want to start a smoothie diet. Whether you want to lose weight, feel incredibly energetic, or just consume more natural vitamins and minerals, drinking a delicious smoothie doesn't have to be hard. It doesn't even have to take longer than 10 minutes! If you're sick of processed foods and chemical-laced junk, then start enjoying nutritious, well-balanced beverages. You'll love how sexy you look and feel when you start a natural diet.

Whatever your reasons, you're reading this book because:
A. you own a blender, and
B. you have no time to cook.

We understand. We're here for you. We want to help.

Sometimes, it seems like no amount of preparation or whole nights spent in our kitchens will get us anywhere. So much planning and cooking, and for what? An okay meal, and a really big mess. Not anymore! In this book, we'll help you:
• Plan shopping ahead, with a list of the must-have ingredients for the majority of the recipes found in this book.

- Get in the habit of planning and freezing for easy, nearly no-chopping meal preparation.
- Follow recipes for new and amazingly simple dishes that you'll love, and that require no more than a couple free hours on a Sunday or some free time in the morning.

Freeze N' Throw

To make your preparation time in the mornings even shorter, set aside ten minutes each weekend to plan ahead your shopping list (for any ingredients that you don't already have ready). This way, you won't be frazzled Monday morning when, half-way through a recipe, you realize you don't have any coconut milk. It's the worst. We've all done it.

To make things even easier on yourself, go ahead and chop up the veggies that you'll need for the week and freeze them! Whether in plastic baggies or resealable plastic containers, it'll be a breeze in the mornings to take what you need out of the freezer, measure it out, and throw it in the slow cooker. That's it!

While some recipes call for "one whole diced onion" or "half of a green pepper", just remember: roughly, a whole pepper or small/medium onion is one cup. When it comes to garlic, one clove is roughly one teaspoon, minced. Over time, you'll become comfortable with eyeballing and knowing how much or how little to use.

Even if you throw in a few more pre-chopped carrots or celery than a recipe calls for, what's the hurt? Extra veggies are always a good thing! Cooking can be a wonderful way to experiment and learn about flavors and measurements, and there's no easier way to cook than blending.

Now, all that's left to do is start! Life is busy and chaotic, but cooking dinner doesn't have to be. With a little planning, a little tossing, and a lot of delicious and satisfying meals, drinking smoothies won't be difficult ever again.

Always Keep Your Home Stocked With These Ingredients:

Fruits	Vegetables	Nuts, Herbs, Oils & Toppings	Liquids
Blueberries	Spinach	Greek yogurt	Coconut milk
Bananas	Kale	Almond butter	Almond milk
Avocados	Celery	Peanut butter	Coconut water
Apples (red & green)	Carrots	Coconut oil	
Strawberries	Ginger	Walnuts	
Pineapples	Beets	Almonds	
Lemons	Cucumbers	Honey	
Peaches	Broccoli	Cinnamon	
Oranges	Beans	Turmeric	
Limes	Romaine lettuce	Chili powder	
Raspberry		Flax seeds	
Tomatoes		Cayenne pepper	
Grapes		Cilantro	
Kiwis		Agave nectar	
Dates		Honey	
		Basil	
		Parsley	
		Cumin	
		butter	
		Shredded cheese	
		Dried oregano	
		Cayenne pepper	
		Thyme	
		Paprika	
		Coriander	

Superfood Guide

Simply put, a superfood is a nutrient-rich substance that is thought to be especially beneficial to health. This list is here to help you make quick decisions about what ingredients to include in your grocery list, but is by no means a comprehensive or exclusive list.

1. **Greek yogurt** -- a thicker and creamier yogurt that has a higher concentration of protein than regular yogurt
2. **Blueberries** -- loaded with vitamin C and powerful antioxidants
3. **Cranberries** -- help fight inflammation and full of antioxidants and vitamin C
4. **Acai berry** -- one of the fruits known to be richest in antioxidants
5. **Strawberries** -- loaded with vitamin C and antioxidants
6. **Flax seeds** -- loaded with omega-3's and lignans that help prevent cancer
7. **Chia seeds** -- contain high amounts of essential fatty acids, magnesium, iron, calcium, and potassium
8. **Kale** -- a bitter green leaf chock full of fiber, calcium, iron, and antioxidants
9. **Broccoli** -- a very mean grean that packs a powerful punch of vitamins, minerals, and fiber
10. **Spinach** -- a superior green leaf that contains high amounts of antioxidants, anti-inflammatories, and vitamins to promote many basic functions (including eye and bone development)
11. **Almonds** -- a very nutrient-dense nut that is loaded with calcium, vitamin E, magnesium, and iron
12. **Ginger** -- more common in Asian cooking, ginger is world-renowned for its anti-inflammatory properties
13. **Carrots** -- world-renowned to fight cardiovascular disease and improve vision systems in the body
14. **Coconut** -- loaded with a unique chain of fatty acids that have powerful positive effects on health, including improved brain function
15. **Dark chocolate** -- celebrate that this substance is loaded with nutrients from the cacao tree, including powerful antioxidants and iron, magnesium, copper, and manganese

Superfood Powders:

It is not necessary to purchase these superfood powders, as some tend to be on the pricey side. But we are including this list here for those who might be interested. You can't put a price on your health.

1. Amazing Grass Green Superfood (www.amazinggrass.com)
2. Incredible Berries (http://www.healthkismet.com/incredible-berries/)
3. Purple Dragon (http://www.healthkismet.com/purple-dragon/)
4. Total Living Drink Greens (http://kyleahealth.com/product/total-living-drink-greens-2)
5. Athletic Greens (https://athleticgreens.com/v5)

(We are not affiliated with any of these brands)

These are just a few our research has turned up as worth trying. You can always shop at stores like Wholefoods or Trader Joe's to find more brands and varieties.

Nutribullet Blender Tips

To get the most out your blender, keep it in a dedicated place in your kitchen. Think of this as your smoothie station, not that smoothies are all you can make with this fantastic device.

If you are new to the Nutribullet, here are some basic rules you MUST remember if you don't want to break your machine:
1. Putting hard vegetables (like carrots) without liquid will get you bad results.
2. Do NOT operate the machine for longer than 1 minute at a time, as you will damage the motor from overheating.
3. If the motor stops working, you MUST unplug the base and let the machine cool for at least an hour before trying to use it again.
4. Make sure that the cord is conveniently stashed away and not exposed to hot surfaces, as this will cause it to melt.
5. Certain fruits have seeds and pits that will release dangerous cyanide into your drinks (usually in small amounts, but daily use can cause serious damage). Some examples are: apple seeds, cherry pits, peach pits, plum pits, apricot pits, etc.
6. Do not run the Nutribullet with empty cups attached, as this can damage the unit.
7. Though this machine can crush some ice with liquid inside, it was not designed to be used solely as an ice crusher.

Easy Cleaning Tips

The Power Base

The Power Base generally won't get dirty, but liquids can lead into it if the lid is not sealed tightly onto the cups. Unplug the base and wipe both the inside and outside with a damp cloth.

Do not submerge the base underwater, or attempt to clean it in the dishwasher.

The Cups

Cleaning the cups is super easy. All you have to do is rinse out whatever food is remaining in the cup and wash it as you would any regular cup -- by hand or in the dishwasher.

If there are thick substances (like peanut butter) that are stuck in there and won't come out, one option is to fill the cup with ⅔ solution of soapy water and screw on the milling blade. Blend this soapy cocktail for about 20-30 seconds to loosen whatever is stuck inside, and rinse everything out.

Some Great Tricks

Flavored ice cubes. You can easily replace regular ice cubes with flavored ones by freezing your favorite fruit juice or tea ahead of time. When it's time to make your smoothie, just throw in these flavored cubes for an enhanced flavor and texture -- while keeping it nice and cold.

Quickly make dips, spreads, and salsas.

Store your creations in jars to preserve them longer.

Easily make food crumbs for pies or as a topping.

Make different sauces and dressings to create a variety of flavors for all your meals throughout the week.

Store your chopped veggies and fruits in frozen bags to get in and out of the kitchen quickly.

Create your own fresh herb spice blends for an infinite number of flavor combinations.

If you get bored of smoothies and juices, you can always make fresh soups that are equally nutritious.

RECIPES

The directions for most of the recipes in this book are pretty simple. Follow this template unless extra directions are provided (check the beginning of each section)

Directions:
1. Add liquid first,then softer ingredients,and harder items like ice last.
2. Blend on medium and increase to high for 30-45 seconds.

I. 100 Smoothie recipes

Directions:
1. Add liquid first,then softer ingredients,and harder items like ice last.
2. Blend on medium and increase to high for 30-45 seconds.

A. 20 Superfood Recipes

① BLUEBERRY FLAX SUPERFOOD SMOOTHIE

Ingredients
- 1 cup blueberries, frozen
- 1 tbsp flaxseed, ground
- Handful of spinach
- ¼ cup full-fat Greek yogurt
- 1 cup coconut milk or any kind of milk

② SUPERFOOD POWER SMOOTHIE

Ingredients
- 2 large bananas, previously peeled, sliced, and frozen
- 1 heaping handful spinach (about 1.5 cups)
- ½ of a large apple, chopped (or 1 small)
- ½ cup almond milk
- 1 tbsp ground flax (optional)
- 7 large strawberries, sliced

❸ MINT CHIP SUPERFOOD SMOOTHIE

Ingredients

- 2-3 frozen bananas
- 1-2 tbsps hemp milk or other non-dairy milk
- 1 tbsp hemp seeds
- ½ to 1 teaspoon spirulina powder
- 2 drops peppermint oil
- 1½ tbsps dark chocolate chips or cocoa nibs, divided

❹ MACA ALMOND CACAO SMOOTHIE

Ingredients

- ¼ cup almond milk
- 2 frozen bananas
- 2 tbsps almond butter
- 1 date cacao beans/nibs
- 1 tbsp coconut oil
- 1 tbsp Maca

❺ VEGAN SUPERFOOD CHOCOLATE SMOOTHIE

Ingredients

- 2 bananas
- 6 ice cubes
- 1 tbsp coconut oil
- 1 tbsp dairy free plain yogurt
- 1 tbsp chia seeds
- 2 tbsp hemp seeds
- 1 tsp camu camu powder
- 1 tsp cacao
- ¼ cup coconut milk (or unsweetened almond milk)

❻ AVOCADO SUPERFOOD SMOOTHIE

Ingredients

- 1 Hass avocado
- 1 ½ cups frozen blueberries
- 3 strawberries
- 17 mint leaves
- 1 ½ cups organic orange juice
- ¼ cup plain yogurt
- 2 tbsps agave nectar
- ½ cup frozen raspberries

❼ GREEN COCONUT SMOOTHIE (HEALTHY)

Ingredients

- 2 bananas, frozen
- 2 big handfuls spinach
- 1 cup milk
- ¼ teaspoon cinnamon
- 1 teaspoon vanilla
- 1 tbsp coconut oil

❽ BANANA BEET SMOOTHIE

Ingredients

- 2 bananas, frozen
- 1 medium sized golden beet
- ¼ cup rolled oats (optional)
- 1 cup unsweetened almond milk
- ½ cup full-fat coconut milk
- ½ teaspoon vanilla extract
- Pinch cinnamon (optional)

9 GREEN SMOOTHIE

Ingredients

- 1 cup hemp milk
- 1 cup kale packed
- 2 cups frozen pineapple
- 2 kiwis, whole
- ½ avocado
- 1 banana
- 1 T. coconut oil
- 1 T. maca powder

10 BERRY BLAST ALMOND SMOOTHIE

Ingredients

- 1 cup unsweetened almond milk
- ¼ cup fat free vanilla Greek yogurt, or a dairy free yogurt
- 2 heaping tbsps protein powder
- about 8 to 10 raw almonds
- 1 tbsp golden flax seeds
- ½ cup blueberries
- 5 or 6 strawberries
- small handful of fresh spinach

11 BLUEBERRY MANGO AND SUPERFOOD SMOOTHIE

Ingredients

- 200 ml organic goat or soy yogurt
- 1 handful frozen blueberries
- 1 handful frozen mango
- 1 tbsp bee pollen
- 1 tbs goji berries
- ½ cup of raw oats or almonds

12 SUPERFOOD PB BANANA AND CACAO GREEN SMOOTHIE

Ingredients

- 3/4 cup unsweetened vanilla almond milk
- 1 loose cup baby spinach
- 2 teaspoons peanut butter
- ½ frozen ripe banana
- 1/3 oz (heaping tbsp) cacao nibs
- 1 cup ice
- (optional) a few drops liquid stevia

13 SUPERFOOD PUMPKIN PIE SMOOTHIE

Ingredients

- 1 frozen banana
- ½ cup Greek yogurt
- ½ teaspoon pumpkin pie spice
- ½ cup almond milk
- 2 tbsps pure maple syrup
- ¼ teaspoon vanilla
- ⅔ cup pumpkin puree
- 1 tbsp flax seeds
- 1 cup ice

⑭ SUPERFOOD CHIA GREEN SMOOTHIE

Ingredients

- 2 cups cold water
- 2 handfuls spinach
- 1 kale leaf, medium
- ½ long English cucumber, sliced
- ½ any apple, chopped and not cored/seeded/peeled
- 2 tbsp chia seeds
- ½ lemon, juice of

⑮ CHOCOLATE-CAULIFLOWER SMOOTHIE RECIPES FROM 'SUPERFOOD SMOOTHIES'

Ingredients

- 1/4 cup Medjool dates, pitted (about 3–4 large fruits)
- 3 cups steamed cauliflower
- 1/4 cup cacao nibs
- 2 tbsp hemp seeds
- 1 tbsp cacao powder
- 1 ½ cups rice milk, original variety
- 2 cups coconut ice
- Sweetener, to taste

⑯ SUPERFOOD TRIPLE BERRY CHIA PUDDING

Ingredients

- 1 cup unsweetened almond/coconut milk beverage
- 3/4 cup fresh blueberries, blackberries and raspberries
- 2 tbsp chia seeds
- 5-6 drops sugar/honey to taste

⑰ CHOCOLATE MALT SUPERFOOD SMOOTHIE

Ingredients

- 2 frozen bananas
- 1½ tbsps maca root powder
- 1 tbsp raw cacao powder or 2 tbsps cocoa powder
- 1 medjool date, pitted
- 1 teaspoon pure vanilla extract
- 2-4 tbsps water
- optional: cacao nibs

⑱ EGGLESS NOG SUPERFOOD SMOOTHIE

Ingredients

- 2 tbsp superfood powder
- 1 cup Vanilla almond Milk
- 2 cups (1 large apple) Apple (chopped)
- 2 whole, pitted Date
- ¼ tsp Nutmeg (ground)
- ½ tsp Vanilla Extract
- ¼ cup Walnuts
- ¼ cup Water
- 1.5 cups Ice

19 SPICY CITRUS AND BERRY SMOOTHIE WITH CHIA SEEDS

Ingredients

- 1 ½ cups freshly squeezed orange juice
- ¼ cup pure mangosteen juice
- 1 ½ cups frozen red raspberries
- 1 ½ cups frozen peach slices
- 1 tbsp chia seeds
- 1 tbsp coconut oil, melted
- Few pinches of cayenne pepper, to taste

20 BLUEBERRY AVOCADO AND SPINACH SUPERFOOD SMOOTHIE

Ingredients

- 1 cup blueberries, frozen or fresh
- 1 cup fresh spinach leaves
- 1 cup almond-coconut milk
- ½ ripe avocado, skinned and pitted
- 1 tbsp chia seeds
- ¼ teaspoon cinnamon
- 1 tbsp honey
- 1 scoop protein powder
- ½ fresh ice

B. 20 High-protein recipes

21 BANANA RASPBERRY CHIA SMOOTHIE

Ingredients

- ½ banana
- ½ cup raspberries
- ½ cup plain Greek yogurt
- 1 tbsp chia seeds
- 1 scoop protein powder
- ½ cup water
- ½ teaspoon cinnamon
- pinch nutmeg
- two handfuls ice - to taste

22 STRAWBERRY BANANA SMOOTHIE WITH CHIA SEEDS

Ingredients

- 1 cup (250 mL) fresh strawberries, hulled and cleaned
- 1 peeled banana, frozen
- 4 cubes of ice
- 1 T chia seeds soaked in ¼ cup (60 mL) of water
- ⅓ cup (160 mL) light coconut milk

23 BLUEBERRY MANGO SMOOTHIE

Ingredients
- 1 cup frozen blueberries
- 1 cup mango chunks
- 1 cup plain Greek yogurt
- ¼ cup vanilla soy milk, almond milk, or skim milk or water

24 PAPAYA GINGER SMOOTHIE

Ingredients
- 1 ½ cups papaya, chilled and cut into chunks
- 1 cup ice
- ½ cup nonfat plain Greek yogurt
- 2 teaspoons fresh ginger, peeled and chopped
- Juice of half a lemon
- 1 teaspoon agave nectar
- Leaves from one sprig of mint

25 PEANUT BUTTER AND JELLY PROTEIN SMOOTHIE

Ingredients
- 1 cup frozen berries
- 1 tbsp all-natural peanut butter
- 1 scoop Vanilla Bean, Designer Whey Sustained Energy
- 2 tbsps rolled oats
- 1 cup soy milk

26 FRENCH TOAST PROTEIN SHAKE

Ingredients
- ½ cup Fat free cottage cheese
- 11 Scoop vanilla protein powder
- 21 tsp Maple extract (or 2 tbs sugar free maple syrup)
- ½ tsp Cinnamon Dash Nutmeg or pumpkin pie spice
- 3-5 Stevia packets
- ½-1 cup Water
- 5-10 ice cubes
- Optional: ½ tsp xanthan gum 3, ½ tsp butter extract

27 CHOCOLATE PEANUT BUTTER PROTEIN SMOOTHIE

Ingredients
- 1 large banana, peeled, sliced,
- and frozen
- 3 tbsps unsweetened cocoa powder
- 6 oz Chobani 0% Greek Yogurt (or 2%, flavored or unflavored)
- 3/4 cup skim milk
- 1 tbsp honey, maple syrup, or agave
- 1 tbsp peanut butter

28 GREEN WARRIOR PROTEIN SMOOTHIE

Ingredients
- ½ cup fresh red grapefruit juice
- 1 cup destemmed dinosaur/lacinato kale
- 1 large sweet apple, cored and roughly chopped
- 1 cup chopped cucumber
- heaping ½ cup chopped celery (1 medium. stalk)
- 3-4 tbsps hemp hearts
- ¼ cup frozen mango
- 1/8 cup fresh mint leaves
- ½ tbsp virgin coconut oil (optional)
- 3-4 ice cubes
- ½-1 tbsp algae oil, optional

29 COCONUT ALMOND PROTEIN SHAKE

Ingredients
- For the nuts:
- 3/4 cup raw almonds
- ¼ cup unsweetened shredded dried coconut
- 2 cups warm water
For the shake:
- 2 cups cold water
- 1 teaspoon kosher or celtic sea salt
- 1 rounded scoop vanilla protein powder (with no added sugar)
- 2 teaspoons grated fresh ginger
- 1 teaspoon ground cinnamon
- 1 teaspoon vanilla extract
- 2 tbsps coconut butter or coconut oil
- Honey, to taste (optional)

30 BLUEBERRY PINEAPPLE OATMEAL SMOOTHIE

Ingredients
- 1 cup fresh blueberries
- 1 banana
- ½ pineapple, chopped into chunks
- 10 ice cubes
- ½ cup almond milk
- ½ cup of rolled oats
- 1 scoop of vanilla protein powder
- ½ cup of Greek yogurt

31 DARK CHOCOLATE PEPPERMINT PROTEIN SHAKE

Ingredients
- 1 large banana, frozen
- 2-3 large ice cubes
- 1 cup non dairy milk of choice
- 1 scoop Chocolate Protein Powder
- 2 tbsps cocoa powder
- Pinch of sea salt
- ¼ tsp pure peppermint extract
- optional add In: 1 tbsp dark/vegan chocolate chips
- optional toppings: homemade whipping cream, vegan whipped topping, or Greek yogurt

32 CHERRY ALMOND SMOOTHIE

Ingredients

- 1 cup of fresh or frozen pitted cherries
- 1 cup of almond or regular milk
- 2 tbsps of almond butter
- 3-4 ice cubes
- 1 scoop vanilla protein powder

33 CHOCOLATE ESPRESSO PROTEIN SMOOTHIE

Ingredients

- 1 banana, chunked and frozen
- 1 scoop chocolate protein powder
- 1 tsp instant coffee grounds {or ½ cup brewed coffee, chilled}
- 1 tsp unsweetened cocoa powder
- 1 tsp coconut palm sugar {optional}
- 1 cup coconut milk {or other milk}
- ½ cup ice {optional}

34 ROASTED STRAWBERRY PROTEIN SMOOTHIE

Ingredients

- 1-½ cups fresh strawberries, quartered
- ½ tbsp raw sugar
- 1/3 cup reduced fat cottage cheese
- ½ cup fat free milk
- 1 cup crushed ice
- 1 tsp chia seeds
- 6 to 8 drops liquid stevia (optional)

35 GREEN VANILLA ALMOND POST-WORKOUT SHAKE

Ingredients

- 1 cup unsweetened coconut milk
- 2 cups baby spinach
- 1 frozen banana
- 2 tbsps almond butter
- 2 teaspoons organic vanilla extract
- ¼ cup (1 scoop) protein powder
- 1 cup ice

36 STRAWBERRY ALMOND PROTEIN DREAM SMOOTHIE

Ingredients

- 1 cup frozen organic strawberries
- 2 dates
- ½ cup almonds, soaked overnight
- ½ cup filtered water

㊗ ORANGE MANGO RECOVERY SMOOTHIE

Ingredients

- 1½ cups unsweetened almond milk
- 1 scoop vanilla vegan protein powder
- 1 cup frozen mango chunks
- 1 navel orange
- 2 tbsp cashews
- 1 tsp cinnamon
- ½ tsp turmeric
- 5 g fermented l-glutamine (optional)

㊳ THE PEANUT BUTTER POWER PROTEIN SHAKE

Ingredients

- 1 Scoop Chocolate Whey
- 2 tbsp. Natural Peanut butter
- ½ Banana
- 1 cup Skim Milk
- ¼ cup Quaker Oats
- 2 ice cubes
- Pinch of Salt

㊴ WINTER MINT CHOCOLATE PROTEIN SHAKE

Ingredients

- 1 Scoop Chocolate or Chocolate Mint Whey Protein Powder
- 1 cup almond Milk
- ½ cup No Sugar Added Mint Chocolate Chip Ice Cream
- Optional, 1 Drop Peppermint Extract

㊵ CHERRY GINGER LIME SMOOTHIE

Ingredients

- 2 cups cherries, fresh or frozen
- 1 cup blueberries, fresh or frozen
- 1 whole lime, peeled
- ⅔ cup plain Greek yogurt
- 2 scoops protein powder
- ½ green apple
- 2 inch piece ginger root, thinly sliced
- 2 tbsps tart cherry juice
- 2 tbsps flax seed
- 1 cup water
- ice to taste

C. 20 Weight-loss recipes

41 FAT BURNING GREEN TEA AND VEGETABLE SMOOTHIE

Ingredients

- 3 Broccoli Florets
- 2 Cauliflower Florets
- 2 Pineapple Spears
- Green tea

42 CRISP APPLE SMOOTHIE

Ingredients

- 1 scoop protein powder
- 1 cup water
- 1 apple, cored, seeded and quartered
- 1 medium orange, peeled and quartered
- 1 banana, sliced
- 2 handfuls spinach
- 1 medium carrot, peeled and sliced

43 4 INGREDIENT GREEN SMOOTHIE

Ingredients

- 2 cups raw spinach
- 2 frozen medium bananas
- 1 cup fresh, whole strawberries
- 1 cup unsweetened vanilla almond milk

44 5 INGREDIENT CREAMY BANANA GREEN SMOOTHIE

Ingredients

- 1 banana
- 1 avocado
- 2 cups(450g) spinach
- 1 green apple
- 1 cup (240 g) Greek yogurt

45 GREEN SUPERFOOD SMOOTHIE

Ingredients

- ½ cup water
- 1½ cups freshly squeezed grapefruit juice
- 2 cups spinach
- 1 tsp spirulina
- 2 kiwis
- 1 avocado
- ½ cup frozen mango chunks

46 TROPICAL GREENS SMOOTHIE

Ingredients

- 1 ½ cups fresh watermelon chunks
- Juice of one lime
- 1 large handful of fresh baby spinach
- 2 sprigs of fresh curly parsley
- 2 sprigs of fresh mint
- ½ cup frozen strawberries
- 1 cup frozen pineapple tidbits
- ½ cup frozen mango chunks
- ½ cup green tea or coconut water

ⓐ BLUEBERRY PINEAPPLE GREEN DETOX SMOOTHIE

Ingredients
- 1 cup baby spinach or baby kale
- 1 cup fresh really ripe pineapple, cored and cut into chunks
- ½ cup plain Greek yogurt non-fat
- 2 teaspoons of ground cinnamon
- dash of turmeric
- 1-2 teaspoons of chia seeds, flaxseed
- 1 small knob the size of a quarter of fresh ginger root
- juice from ½ lemon
- ½ cup water, milk or juice
- 2 cups frozen blueberries

ⓑ RASPBERRY MANGO CHIA SEED SMOOTHIE

Ingredients
- 1 cup apple juice frozen concentrate
- 1. 5 cups frozen raspberries
- 1.5 cup frozen mango chunks
- 2 cups spinach
- 2 Tbs Chia seeds
- Water

ⓒ TROPICAL GREEN SMOOTHIE

Ingredients
- 1 medium mango, peeled and cubed
- 2 cups watermelon, cubed
- 1 large kale leaf or spinach
- ½ cup freshly squeezed orange juice
- 1 cup coconut water
- ¼ teaspoon freshly ground black pepper
- a few mint leaves

ⓓ RAINBOW SMOOTHIE

Ingredients
- Layer 1 Banana/almond:
- 130g crushed ice2 small bananas (about 80g each with skin removed)
- 10 almonds
- 50ml semi skimmed milk
- Layer 2 Kale/date:
- 50g crushed ice
- 2 medjool dates, stones removed and roughly chopped
- 75g kale
- Layer 3 blueberry
- 80g crushed ice
- 70g blueberries
- 50ml water
- Layer 4 Strawberry/milk
- 80g crushed ice
- 80g strawberries, green bits cut off
- 50ml semi skimmed milk

51 FRUITY GREEN SMOOTHIE

Ingredients

- ½ large bunch of kale, stems removed
- 2 cups pineapple rings
- 1 mango
- 1 ripe banana (optional)
- 1-2 cups water
- coconut water

52 VERY CHERRY GREEN SMOOTHIE

Ingredients

- 1 cup frozen cherries
- ½ cup frozen mango chunks
- 2 cups organic spinach
- 100% baby kale
- 1 banana
- 2 cups pomegranate-blueberry juice

53 CREAMY AVOCADO KALE SMOOTHIE

Ingredients

- ½ an Avocado
- ½ cup Kale
- 1 TBSP cacao Nibs
- ½ cup Greek Yogurt
- ½ cup Vanilla almond Milk
- ½ cup Frozen Mango
- 2 tsp Honey

54 BERRIES AND OATS SMOOTHIE

Ingredients

- 12 ounces coconut water
- 2 small oranges (or 1 large)
- 1 cup blueberries
- 2 cups strawberries
- 2 cups spinach
- 1 medium banana
- 2 cups ice (less if using frozen fruit)
- ½ cup rolled oats

55 GREEN BLUEBERRY BANANA SMOOTHIE

Ingredients

- 1 cup skim milk (or milk of choice)
- 1/3 cup plain nonfat Greek yogurt
- 1 frozen banana
- 3/4 cup frozen blueberries
- 1 cup baby spinach
- 1 T. flaxseed meal
- 4 t. maple syrup or honey
- ½ t. vanilla extract
- 1 T. unsweetened shredded coconut (optional)

56 LULU'S GREEN SMOOTHIE

Ingredients

- A big fistful of baby spinach or baby kale (roughly 1 cup packed)
- 1 ripe banana, cold
- ¼ avocado, cold
- 2 cups original or vanilla soymilk
- Optional: fresh mint leaves or a dash cinnamon
- 2-3 ice cubes

57 BLUEBERRY PEACH KALE CHIA SMOOTHIE

Ingredients

- 2 cups coconut milk or almond milk
- 2 cups blueberries (fresh or frozen)
- 1 cup peaches (fresh or frozen)
- 1 cup kale
- 1 small banana (fresh or frozen)
- 1 tbsp Chia seeds
- 1 tbsp honey
- 1 ½ cups ice (less if using frozen fruit)

58 GREEN SMOOTHIE BOWL

Ingredients

- 1 handful of baby spinach leaves
- 1 handful of baby kale leaves
- 2 medium sized carrots
- 1 large very ripe banana
- 1 cup of blueberries
- 2 tbsps of hemp protein powder
- 1/3 cup of unsweetened almond milk
- 1 tbsp of almond butter

59 GRAPE MANGO KALE SMOOTHIE

Ingredients

- 8 ounces coconut water
- ½ cup red grapes
- ½ cup watermelon
- 1 cup mango, fresh or frozen
- 1 cup kale
- 1 carrot, cut into chunks
- juice of ½ lemon
- 1 date
- 1 ½ cups of ice

60 GREEN GOODNESS IN A GLASS

Ingredients

- 1 Green Apple
- 2 Beetroot Leaves
- 2-3 Kale Leaves
- ½ Small Avocado
- Ice cubes

- Lots of Cinnamon
- 5 cm Piece of Cucumber
- Milk of choice (rice, almond, soy, coconut water or just water.)

D. 10 Anti-aging recipes

61 BLUEBERRY PEACH ANTI AGING SMOOTHIE

Ingredients
- ½ cup fresh or frozen blueberries
- 1½ cup fresh sliced peach, with peel or frozen peaches, pits removed
- About ¾ cup unsweetened vanilla almond milk, to the fill line

62 ANTI-AGING TURMERIC SMOOTHIE

Ingredients
- 1 cup coconut milk
- ½ cup frozen pineapple or mango chunks
- 1 fresh banana
- 1 tbsp coconut oil
- 1 teaspoon turmeric
- ½ teaspoon cinnamon
- ½ teaspoon ginger
- ½ avocado

63 CHOCOLATE BERRY ALMOND BLAST

Ingredients
- 1 cup Spinach
- 1 tbsp cacao Nibs
- 1 tbsp almond butter
- ½ cup Cherries, frozen
- ½ cup Mixed Berries
- 1 Splash Vanilla
- ½ teaspoon Ceylon Cinnamon
- 1 ½ cups almond Milk

64 BLUEBERRY DETOX SMOOTHIE

Ingredients
- 1 cup wild frozen blueberries, or just frozen blueberries
- 1 cup cubed raw red beets, peeled
- 1 cup cubed watermelon
- 1 cup coconut water
- 1 teaspoon chia seeds (optional)
- 1 handful of basil leaves (or mint)

65 ALKALINE CLEANSING SMOOTHIE

Ingredients
- 1 rib of celery
- ¼ cucumber
- 1 handful of cilantro
- 1 handful of parsley
- ½ lemon, peeled
- A slice of ginger

66 TANGERINE TURMERIC ANTIOXIDANT SMOOTHIE

Ingredients

- 2 tangerines, peeled
- 1 large organic carrot, unpeeled
- ½ avocado
- 1 cup coconut milk
- 1 teaspoon turmeric
- 1 teaspoon Dole milled chia seeds
- 5-6 ice cubes
- Cut carrot into large chunks. Add all ingredients to a blender or Vitamix and process until smooth.

67 RED GRAPE. PLUM. AND RASPBERRY ANTIOXIDANT SMOOTHIE

Ingredients

- 1 cup red seedless grapes
- 2 handfuls spinach
- 3 red plums, pits removed
- ½ cup raspberries

70 WATERMELON SMOOTHIE

Ingredients

- 1½ cups Watermelon (seedless or remove seeds)
- 1 frozen banana
- 1 apple, peeled and cored

68 AN ANTI-AGING SMOOTHIE

Ingredients

- 1 ½ cup Kale Cut Up
- 2 Celery Sticks
- 1 Juice Whole Lemon
- 1 Medium Apple (Cored)
- 1 handful Parsley
- 1 ½ cup coconut Water

69 CO. CO. COIT BLAST

Ingredients

- 1 Banana
- 1 tbsp cacao
- ¼ cup Goji Berries
- ½ cup Grapes
- ½ cup Blueberries
- 1 tbsp Honey
- 3 ice cubes
- To Max Line Water

- ¾ cup fat free Thick Greek Yogurt
- Agave or honey

E. 10 Detoxification recipes

71 DETOX SMOOTHIE
Ingredients
- 1 frozen sliced very ripe banana, previously peeled & sliced
- ¼ cup almond milk
- 1 and ¼ cups chopped pineapple
- 1 peach, peeled and sliced
- ½ cup Greek yogurt
- 1 - 2 cups fresh spinach
- Juice + zest of 1 lime, optional (provides great flavor)

72 DETOX BLUEBERRY FRUIT SMOOTHIE
Ingredients
- ½ cup frozen blueberries
- ¼ cup unsweetened cranberry juice
- 1-2 bananas

73 CITRUS & GREEN TEA DETOX SMOOTHIE
Ingredients
- 1 navel orange
- 1 grapefruit
- the juice of half a lemon
- ½ cup of unsweetened green tea, chilled
- ½ cup of nonfat Greek yogurt
- ½ a frozen banana
- 1 cup of ice
- ½ tbsp honey
- optional garnishes:
- orange/grapefruit/lemon zest on top

74 LEMON GINGER DETOX DRINK
Ingredients
- 1 12-ounce glass water, at room temperature
- Juice of ½ lemon
- ½ inch knob of ginger root

75 DETOX BEET AND CARROT SMOOTHIE
Ingredients
- 1 carrot, peeled, sliced
- 1 beet, peeled, sliced
- ½ cup red grapes
- 1 clementine, peeled
- 1 slice of ginger, peeled, about the size of a quarter
- ½ cup green tea

76 GRAPEFRUIT-CADO SUNRISE SMOOTHIE
Ingredients
- ½ avocado
- ½ cup fresh squeezed orange juice
- 1 cup fresh squeezed grapefruit juice
- 1 cup DOLE frozen strawberries
- 3/4 cup DOLE banana (use frozen banana slices for thicker smoothie)
- ¼ cup ice
- optional: 1 tsp maple syrup

77 NATURAL DAILY DETOX REMEDY DRINK

Ingredients

- 16-25 oz Cold Water
- 1-2 tbsp Apple Cider Vinegar
- 1 Full Lemon
- Ice
- Optional:
- Cinnamon
- Stevia

78 MATCHA MANGO PINEAPPLE SMOOTHIE

Ingredients

- 1.25 tsp matcha green tea
- 1 scoop protein powder
- some honey
- 1 c frozen mango chunks
- 1 tbsp pineapple juice
- 1 c pineapple
- ½ to 1 c water

79 SPRING CLEANING DETOX

Ingredients

- 1 teaspoon of whole flax seeds.
- 1 red apple, peeled and sliced.
- 8 snack-sized peeled carrots (or 2 normal carrots, peeled and chopped).
- ¼ inch nub of fresh ginger root, skin removed. (should be moist)
- 1 cup of lukewarm water.

80 CRANBERRY BLISS DETOX SMOOTHIE

Ingredients

- 2 apples, sliced, peel left on
- 2 pears, sliced, peel left on
- 1 lemon, peeled, cut in quarters, seeds removed
- 1 cup fresh cranberries
- 2 cups of filtered water
- Sweetener of choice
- 4-6 Ice cubes
- 1 tbsp turmeric
- 2 teaspoons pumpkin pie spice blend (optional) OR 2 teaspoons of cinnamon or 1 teaspoon of nutmeg

F. 10 Energy boosting recipes

81 AFTERNOON ENERGY SMOOTHIE

Ingredients

- 2 medium bananas (Peeled)
- 3 whole Medjool dates (Pits removed)
- 1 cup unsweetened almond milk
- 1 TBSP hulled hemp seeds
- ½ cup ice (optional)

82 ENERGY BOOST FRUIT SMOOTHIE

Ingredients
- 1 cup of pineapple, peeled and chopped
- 1 medium orange, peeled
- 1 cup raspberries
- 1 medium banana, peeled
- 1 cup almond milk
- 1 cup crushed ice

83 BLUEBERRY ALMOND BUTTER SMOOTHIES

Ingredients
- 1 banana, peeled
- 1 cup frozen blueberries
- ½ cup almond butter
- ½ cup plain yogurt
- 3/4 cup almond milk
- 3 dates, pitted and quartered
- 1 cup ice, or as needed

84 FRUIT AND VEGGIE SMOOTHIE

Ingredients
- 2 carrots
- 3 tomatoes
- 2 apples
- 1 cucumber
- 3 slices of pineapple
- 4 beets
- chunk of ginger
- lemon
- 2 bell peppers

85 MANGO-STRAWBERRY WATERMELON SMOOTHIE

Ingredients
- 1 peeled and sliced Mango
- 6-10 Strawberries depending on tartness
- 3-4 cups chopped Watermelon
- 1 tbsp Honey (optional)

86 RAW MANGO LASSI LOVE

Ingredients
- 2 Large fresh ripe organic Mangoes
- 1 banana
- ½ cup of organic hemp hearts (can substitute coconut meat instead)
- 1 teaspoon of chai spice.
- 1 cup of either almond milk, coconut milk, or coconut water.

87 DR. OZ'S ENERGY BOOST SMOOTHIE

Ingredients
- 2 tbsp. pure cocoa powder
- 2 tbsp creamy natural peanut butter
- 1 medium ripe banana
- 8 oz nonfat vanilla Greek yogurt
- ½ cup almond Milk
- 4 to 6 ice cubes
- ½ tsp cinnamon

88 LUSH CHERRY AND COCONUT SMOOTHIE

Ingredients

- ½ cup pitted cherries, frozen or fresh
- ¼ cup (30 g / 1 oz / handful) frozen raspberries
- Juice + flesh from 1 young coconut
- 2 tbsps Healthy Chef Pure Native WPI
- 1 teaspoon chia seed

89 KIWI & GREEN TEA SMOOTHIE

Ingredients

- Makes 4 cups (500 ml)
- 2 cups (500 ml) maché salad (also called lamb's lettuce, valerian, corn salad)
- 2 kiwi
- 1 ½ banana, frozen
- 1 cup pineapple (250 ml)
- 1 cup green tea, cold (250 ml)

90 PEANUT BUTTER AND BANANA OATMEAL SMOOTHIE

Ingredients

- 1 banana
- 1 cup plain yogurt
- 2 tbsp. peanut butter
- ½ cup milk
- ¼ cup quick-cooking oats and a squirt of honey to taste.

G. 10 High-calorie recipes (to stay full longer)

91 STRAWBERRY MANGO AND ALMOND SMOOTHIE

Ingredients

- 1 cup strawberries (fresh or frozen)
- ½ cup mango
- 3-4 almonds (soaked overnight)
- coconut milk to the fill line
- 1 teaspoon honey

92 RASPBERRY CHEESECAKE SMOOTHIE

Ingredients

- ½ cup skim milk
- ½ cup nonfat cottage cheese
- 2 tbsps honey
- ½ tsp vanilla extract
- 1 cup raspberries

93 SWEET POTATO AND BANANA PIE SMOOTHIE

Ingredients
- 2 cups *Water*
- 1 cup of *Sweet Potato*/ One Small Sweet potato (Raw or cooked)
- 4 *Bananas* (4 cups)
- ½ cup *Raisins* / Sultanas (or any dried fruit)
- ¼ cup *Pecans* (Or any other nuts or plain seeds)
- 1 teaspoon *Cinnamon*
- ¼ cup Dried *coconut* (Or any other type of coconut)
- *TO MAKE INTO A GREEN THICKIE* Add:
- 1 cup *Spinach*, tightly packed or 2 cups loosely packed.

94 TROPICAL PROTEIN SHAKE SMOOTHIE

Ingredients
- 1 cup fresh pineapple
- 1 medium kiwi, skin intact
- 2 T unsweetened coconut
- 6 almonds
- 1 cup vanilla Greek yogurt
- coconut milk to the fill line

95 MORNING ENERGY BLAST

Ingredients
- 1 Banana
- 2 tbsps Peanut butter
- ½ cup Greek Yogurt
- 2 tbsps cacao
- 1 Dash Cinnamon
- ice cubes
- To Max Line Water

96 ALMOND BUTTER ME UP!

Ingredients
- 1 Handful Spinach
- ½ Bananas
- 1 tbsp almond butter
- 1 Handful Mixed Berries
- 1 tbsp SuperFood Protein Boost
- To Max Line coconut Water

97 ENERGY BLAST CITRUS GREEN SMOOTHIE

Ingredients
- 2 big handfuls of fresh spinach
- 2 large oranges (or 4 clementines)
- 1 large red grapefruit
- 1 ½ cups of water, orange or grapefruit juice.
- 1 tbsp of Chia Seeds

98 PINEAPPLE GINGER ENERGY BLAST

Ingredients
- 1 cup Spinach
- 1 Small Banana
- ½ cup Greek Yogurt
- 1 tbsp Ginger
- 1 cup Pineapple
- ice cubes
- To Max Line Water

99 ALMOND DELIGHT

Ingredients

- 1 cup Mixed Greens
- ½ cup Raspberries
- ½ cup Strawberries
- ½ cup Garbanzo Beans
- 1 tbsp almond butter
- 2 tbsps SuperFood Protein Boost
- ½ teaspoon Cinnamon
- To Max Line Water

100 CHOCOLATE-COVERED CHERRY SMOOTHIE

Ingredients

- 3/4 cup frozen dark sweet cherries
- 1 cup 35-calorie almond milk
- 1 scoop CytoSport 100% Whey Protein
- 1 tbsp unsweetened cocoa powder
- 1/3 cup baby carrots (optional)
- For the topping
- ½ cup whipping cream
- 1 package Stevia

II. 100 Juice recipes

❶ CARROT. PEAR. RASPBERRY. CUCUMBER JUICE

Ingredients

- 4 or 5 carrots
- 1 pear
- 12 ounces of organic raspberries
- 1 cucumber

❷ PINKY PROMISE ME CARROT JUICE

Ingredients

- 3 organic carrots
- 1 apple
- ½ inch piece of ginger
- a few sprigs of parsley

❸ BEET GREEN. CARROT. APPLE. ORANGE JUICE

Ingredients
- 5 peeled carrots
- 1 bunch beet greens (about 5-6 large), can also use chard
- 2 small oranges, peeled and and cut into half through the equator, seeds removed
- 2 apples, cut into quarters, cores removed

❹ THE ULTIMATE GREEN POWER JUICE

Ingredients
- 6 large Fuji or Gala apples, quartered
- 4 cups baby spinach leaves
- 1 bunch of parsley
- 2 inches fresh ginger, skin removed
- 1 lemon

❺ LAUREN'S FAVORITE GREEN JUICE

Ingredients
- 2 cups baby spinach {packed full}
- ½ english cucumber, peeled
- 3 fuji apples
- 2 navel oranges
- 1 ruby red grapefruit
- 1 small lemon, peeled {optional}

❻ V8 JUICE

Ingredients
- 1 tbsp extra virgin olive oil
- 5 medium-large tomatoes, chopped
- ½ onion, chopped
- 2 cloves garlic
- 1 beet, chopped
- 1 carrot, chopped
- 1 tbsp honey
- 1 dash tabasco sauce
- 1 dash worcestershire sauce
- salt & pepper
- 2 small cucumbers, chopped
- ¼ cup fresh parsley

❼ GRAPEFRUIT VEGGIE LIME JUICE

Ingredients
- 1 pink grapefruit, peeled, sliced
- 2 celery stalks, chopped
- 1 red pepper, cored, stem removed
- ½ lime, skin removed

❽ GRAPEFRUIT MINT JUICE
Ingredients
- 2 grapefruits, peeled and sectioned to fit into the juicer
- 8-10 leaves of fresh mint

⑨ CARROT, ORANGE, AND GINGER JUICE WITHOUT JUICER

Ingredients
- 6 carrots, peeled and cut into large chunks
- 1 orange, peeled and cut into large chunks
- ½-inch piece of fresh ginger root, peeling removed
- 1 cup water
- ice

⑩ GREEN JUICE WITHOUT A JUICER

Ingredients
- 3 handfuls of kale (or about 3 loosely packed cups)
- 1 whole apple, cored and cut into large chunks
- 1 stalk of celery, cut into large chunks
- ½ English cucumber, cut into large chunks
- juice from ½ a lime
- 1 handful of parsley or about 1 cup loosely packed
- 1 cup water
- ice

⑪ WATERMELON RASPBERRY LIME JUICE

Ingredients
- ½ smallish watermelon, seedless
- 3 - 4 ounces raspberries
- 2 limes, freshly squeezed

⑫ BEET HAPPY JUICE

Ingredients
- 3 whole beets, stems removed & cut in half
- 1 green apple – quartered & seeded
- ½ lemon
- thumb size of ginger

⑬ WATERMELON JUICE

Ingredients
- 1 small sweet, organic watermelon
- (a 6 pounder will do)
- 1 small lime, juiced

⑭ GREEN JUICE IN A BLENDER

Ingredients
- 1 ½ cups water
- 2 cups kale
- 2 green apples, cored
- ½ cup parsley leaves
- 1 medium cucumber, quartered
- 2 celery stalks, roughly chopped
- 1 (1-inch) piece of ginger, peeled
- 2 tbsps lemon juice

15 FRESH STRAWBERRY JUICE WITH COCONUT WATER

Ingredients
- 3 cups fresh organic strawberries, stems removed
- 1 organic pear, cored and seeded
- ¼ fresh lime
- small piece of ginger
- ½ cup coconut water

16 PURPLE RAIN DETOX JUICE

Ingredients
- 2 Fuji Apples
- 1 Beet with stalk
- 3 Kale Leaves
- 1 Cucumber

17 GINGER CUCUMBER DETOX JUICE

Ingredients
- 2 cucumbers
- 2 inch knob of ginger
- ½ lime
- 1 cup of parsley
- dash of cayenne pepper

18 PINA COLADA PINEAPPLE DETOX JUICE

Ingredients
- One third of a large pineapple (about 400g)
- 2 apples
- 2 peaches
- A thumb sized piece of root ginger

19 HOLLY'S GREEN JUICE

Ingredients
- 1 cucumber, peeled
- 1 handful of baby kale, or 1 kale stalk with stalk removed
- 1 handful of baby spinach
- 1 crown of broccoli
- 3 gala apples, peeled

20 PEAR AND CARROT DETOX JUICE

Ingredients
- 2 pears (cored)
- 2 carrots
- 2 stalks celery
- 2 nectarines (pits removed)
- 1 lemon (remove the rind leaving most of the white on)
- 2 cups honeydew melon cubed
- 1 orange (remove rind leaving most of the white on)
- 1 inch piece ginger

21 GREEN JUICE

Ingredients
- 2 bunches of curly kale
- 4 Fuji Apples
- 2 Lemons, skin removed
- 2 large cucumbers
- 1.5-2 inch slice of ginger, skin removed

22 GINGER BEET JUICE

Ingredients
- 2 Small Beets (1.5 lbs) & the Beet Greens
- 2 Large Apples (the sweeter the better)
- 1 Small Lime
- 2 Clementines
- 1 Piece Fresh Ginger (about the size of your thumb)
- 1-2 Carrots (optional)

23 KALE GRAPE GINGER LEMON JUICE

Ingredients
- 1 bunch organic kale
- 1 cup organic grapes
- 1 slice ginger, optional
- juice of one lemon wedge

24 PEACHY KEEN

Ingredients
- 4 Sprigs Fresh Basil
- ½ - 1 Lemon
- 4 Peaches
- 8-10 Carrots

25 FENNEL & APPLE DETOX GREEN JUICE

Ingredients
- 1 bunch of spinach, washed (10 ounces)
- 1 bunch of mint
- 1 cucumber
- 2 green apples, cored
- 1 fennel bulb
- ½ lemon

26 ORANGE CREAM JUICE

Ingredients
- 1 small Sweet Potato
- 2 large Carrots
- 3 Clementines (peeled)
- ½ cup almond Milk (original or vanilla)

27 RICKI HELLER'S CRANBERRY-POMEGRANATE HOLIDAY DETOX JUICE

Ingredients
- 4-6 large leaves kale
- 1 cup pomegranate arils (from one large ripe pomegranate)
- 1 cup fresh or frozen cranberries (if frozen, thaw before juicing)
- 1 pear, cored
- 1 knob (about 1 inch or 2.5 cm) fresh ginger, peeled
- 6-12 leaves of fresh mint, optional
- stevia, to taste

28 CARROT GINGER JUICE

Ingredients
- 2 cups chopped and peeled carrots (about four large carrots)
- 2 cups cold water
- 4 tbsps chopped and peeled fresh ginger root (about one three inch piece)
- 1 tbsp fresh lemon juice (the juice of half of one small lemon)

㉙ BROCCOLI JUICE

Ingredients
- 4 carrots (smaller)
- 6 strawberries
- 1 broccoli stalk

㉚ CLASSIC BEET JUICE

Ingredients
- 1 red beet, peel on, chopped
- 1 fuji apple, cored and chopped (peel on)
- 1 kale leaf, stem removed and discarded
- 1 orange, peeled and squeezed
- 1 teaspoon orange rind
- 1 teaspoon grated ginger
- 1-½ cups coconut water

㉛ PLUM AND GINGER DETOX JUICE

Ingredients
- 6 to 8 cup of plums, deseeded and chopped
- 2 inch piece of ginger, chopped
- 1 teaspoon of kala namak or black salt
- honey or sugar to taste

㉜ GREEN JUICE FOR BEGINNERS

Ingredients
- 4 black dino kale leaves
- 1/3 pineapple
- 2 red delicious apples
- 1 lime
- 1" knob of ginger
- 1 handful Italian parsley

㉝ LEAN & MEAN GREEN JUICE

Ingredients
- 5 romaine leaves
- 5 kale leaves
- 1 cucumber, peeled
- ½ bunch parsley
- 3 celery stalks
- 1 cup green grapes

㉞ PRIMAVERA GREEN JUICE

Ingredients
- 2 green apples, halved and quartered
- 4 stalks celery
- 1 cucumber, peeled
- 6 romaine leaves
- 5 kale leaves
- 1 lemon, peeled

㉟ POPEYE POTION

Ingredients
- 2 very large fistfuls of spinach
- ½ cucumber
- 2 apples
- thumb size piece ginger
- ½ lemon

㊱ PINEAPPLE GREEN JUICE

Ingredients
- 1 cup Pineapple
- 1 Granny Smith Apple
- 1 Large Broccoli Stalk and florets
- 5 Kale Leaves
- 1 cup Spinach
- Large handful Fresh Mint

⅜ GREEN GODDESS JUICE

Ingredients
- 2 cups pineapple, cut into chunks (½ a small pineapple)
- 1 ½ cups broccoli, cut into chunks
- 1 large cucumber, sliced
- 3 handfuls of spinach
- 1 handful of mint
- 1 lemon, juice reserved

⅜ BEET COCONUT JUICE AND JUICING WITHOUT A JUICER

Ingredients
- 1 red beet, peel on, chopped
- 1 fuji apple, cored and chopped (peel on)
- 1 la;e leaf, stem removed and discarded
- 1 orange, peeled and squeezed
- 1 teaspoon orange rind
- 1 teaspoon grated ginger
- 1-½ cups coconut water

⅜ GREEN JUICE 11

Ingredients
- ½ red grapefruit
- about 4 chunks of pineapple
- handful of spinach
- handful of parsley
- 2 large stick of celery

⅜ SWEET FREEDOM'S GREEN JUICE

Ingredients
- 2 carrots
- 2 green apples
- 2 kiwis
- ½ a cucumber
- 2-3 handfuls of spinach
- a small bunch of kale or swiss chard, or any green really
- 2-3 leaves of romaine lettuce
- 1 lemon
- a nub of ginger, peeled
- water to dilute (optional)

⅜ FEEL BETTER GREEN JUICE

Ingredients
- 1 green apple, seeds removed
- 1 orange, peeled
- 1 stalk celery
- ½" piece of fresh ginger
- 1 large carrot
- Freshly squeezed lemon juice to taste

⅜ STAY HEALTHY GREEN JUICE

Ingredients
- 3 leaves kale
- 1 apple, core removed
- ½ inch fresh ginger
- 1 cup spinach
- 1 small cucumber
- Juice of ½ lemon
- 4 sprigs cilantro
- 1 cup water

43 HIPPIE JUICE

Ingredients

- 1 cup Watermelon juice
- ⅓ cup kale
- ⅓ cup coconut water
- 4 scoops Pink Lemonade mix
- Water
- Strawberries

44 CARROT APPLE GLOW JUICE

Ingredients

- 2 large organic carrots, tops trimmed
- 1 organic Granny Smith apple, cut into quarters
- 1 Navel orange, quartered and peeled

45 BEET & BERRY LIVER CLEANSE JUICE

Ingredients

- 2 medium beets
- 2 c. blueberries
- 1 apple
- 2 large carrots
- ½ c. raw broccoli
- 1 whole lemon
- 2" knob ginger, skin removed
- ½-1 c. pure coconut water

46 GRAPEFRUIT STRAWBERRY JUICE

Ingredients

- 3 grapefruits, lightly peeled
- 2 cups strawberries, roughly chopped
- 2 tbsp Stevia powder,
- or sweetener of choice

47 BEET CARROT LEMON APPLE KALE CELERY GINGER JUICE

Ingredients

- 2 beets
- 3 carrots
- 1 lemon
- 1 apple
- 5 kale leaves
- 4 stalks celery
- 1 inch ginger

48 PINEAPPLE GINGER PARADISE

Ingredients

- ½ a pineapple, skin cut off with a kitchen knife
- ½ a ripe mango, peeled
- 1 apple
- ½ a lime (skin on)
- 1" piece of peeled fresh ginger

49 BEETROOT JUICE

Ingredients
- 1 small beetroot
- 1 stalk of celery
- 2 carrots
- 1 apple
- 2 leaves of Kale

50 BUSY BEE DETOX JUICE

Ingredients
- 2 medium carrots
- 1 lemon - peeled
- 1" piece of ginger
- 1 stalk of celery
- ½ an apple
- 2 tbsp unfiltered apple cider vinegar
- 1 tsp organic bee pollen*

51 MIDNIGHT JUICE

Ingredients
- 1 cup Pomegranate Seeds
- 1 cup Cranberries
- 2 Valencia Oranges, peeled
- 1 Lime

52 EVERYDAY DETOX JUICE

Ingredients
- 1 quarter fresh pineapple
- 1 orange
- ½ handful cilantro
- ½ small jalapeño, seede

53 GREEN DETOX JUICE

Ingredients
- 3 large kale leaves, washed
- ½ inch chunk of fresh ginger, peeled
- 2 celery stalks, washed
- ½ cup fresh parsley
- 1 small lemon (or ½ large lemon), peeled
- 1 cucumber, washed
- 2 small pears (or one large), washed and cored

54 LIVER DETOX JUICE

Ingredients
- 2 small beets
- 1 fennel bulb
- 2 carrots
- 1 lime

55 BLOOD ORANGE CHILI JUICE

Ingredients
- 6 Blood Oranges
- 2 Serrano Chili
- Agave Nectar

56 PINEAPPLE DETOX JUICE

Ingredients
- 2-3 thick slices of fresh pineapple (the canned kind has tons of added sugars)
- ½ cucumber
- ⅓ cup aloe vera juice
- ½ cup coconut water

57 SPINACH SHOTS

Ingredients
- 3 large handfuls spinach
- ⅓ of a lemon, with peel (if it's organic)
- 1 green apple

58 RED REVIVER

Ingredients
- 1 carrot
- 1 small beet
- 1 small ripe tomato
- 1 - 2 ½ inch wedge red cabbage
- ½ red bell pepper
- ¾ cup diced fresh pineapple
- 1 packet Monk Fruit In The Raw
- ½ cup cold water (optional)

59 ORANGE BROCCOLI JUICE

Ingredients
- 2 apples
- 1 stalk broccoli
- 4 carrots

60 GREEN GUNSLINGER

Ingredients
- 2 peeled kiwi
- 2 green apples
- 1 cucumber
- 1 cup fresh spinach

61 RHUBARB JUICE

Ingredients
- 2 pounds rhubarb stalks
- 8 cups water

62 CRANBERRY POMEGRANATE AND KALE JUICE

Ingredients
- 4-6 large leaves kale
- 1 cup pomegranate arils (from one large ripe pomegranate)
- 1 cup fresh or frozen cranberries (if frozen, thaw before juicing)
- 1 pear, cored
- 1 knob (about 1 inch or 2.5 cm) fresh ginger, peeled
- 6-12 leaves of fresh mint, optional
- stevia, to taste

63 SPICED APPLE CIDER JUICE

Ingredients
- 3 large apples, cored and chopped
- ½ teaspoon of ground cinnamon
- ¼ teaspoon of ground nutmeg

64 TOMATO WITH A KICK

Ingredients
- 2 tomatoes
- 2 green lettuce leaves
- 2 radishes
- 4 parsley sprigs
- ½ lemon

65 ENERGIZER BUNNY ON CRACK JUICE

Ingredients
- 3 kale leaves and stalk
- ½ cucumber
- ½ cup spinach
- 3 stalks of celery
- ¼ fennel bulb
- ¼ head of romaine lettuce (or napa cabbage)
- 1-2 apples
- ½ inch ginger

66 SWEET CURB APPETITE JUICE

Ingredients
- 1 large sweet potato
- 2-3 carrots
- 1 orange
- ¼ pineapple (about 1 cup chopped pineapples)
- optional: squeeze half a lemon in

67 GREEN GUT BEGONE!

Ingredients
- 5 celery stalks
- 2 kale stalks
- 6-8 romaine leaves (or napa cabbage)
- 1 apple
- palmful of parsley
- ½ knob of ginger

68 BEET BLOOD INFUSION JUICE

Ingredients
- ½ small beet
- 3 chard leaves (or kale)
- 2 cucumbers
- 1 apple
- pinch of cayenne pepper

69 STRONG CORE JUICE

Ingredients
- 2 cups spinach
- 1 broccoli floret
- 1 cucumber
- handful of parsley
- 1 lemon
- ½ inch ginger

70 MEAN GREEN JUICE

Ingredients
- 1 cucumber
- 4 celery stalks
- 2 apples
- 6-8 leaves kale
- ½ lemon
- 1 in (2.5 cm) piece of ginger

71 BRIGHT-EYED GREEN JUICE

Ingredients
- 5 small carrots
- 1 large cucumber
- 3 handfuls cilantro
- 2 handfuls kale
- 1 small lime

72 IRON AND VITAMIN C BOOSTING GREEN JUICE

Ingredients

- ½ field cucumber
- 1 cup green grapes
- ½ cup spinach
- 2 small kiwis
- 1-2 cups of water

73 SKIN REJUVENATING GREEN JUICE

Ingredients

- 1 cup blackberries
- 4 sprigs mint
- ½ fennel bulb with greens
- 2 stalks kale
- 2 small green apples
- 1 cup broccoli
- 1 handful watercress
- 1 small cucumber
- 1 lemon, peeled

74 LEAN GREEN POWER JUICE

Ingredients

- ½ pineapple, peeled, cored and chopped
- ½ english cucumber, peeled and chopped
- ½ ripe pear, peeled, cored and chopped
- juice from 1 lime
- 1 cup baby spinach leaves
- 10 mint leaves, chopped
- 1 tsp agave nectar
- crushed ice

75 FAT DISSOLVER JUICE

Ingredients

- 1 pink grapefruit, peeled
- 2 oranges, peeled
- 1 bunch mint
- 1 head romaine lettuce

76 HEALTHY COLADA GREEN JUICE RECIPE

Ingredients

- 1 cucumber
- 1 heart of romaine lettuce
- 3 celery sticks
- 4 cups ripe pineapple
- 1-inch piece ginger
- ½ cup coconut water

77 THINK GREEN JUICE

Ingredients

- 1 celery stalk with leaves, chopped
- 1 green apple, cored and chopped
- 2 large kale leaves, stems removed
- 1 cucumber, chopped
- ½ inch piece of ginger, chopped
- handful of spinach leaves
- handful of mint leaves
- juice of 2 limes
- 2 teaspoons stevia (or raw sugar)
- ¼ teaspoon salt flakes
- 600ml cold water
- 1 teaspoon spirulina powder (optional)

78 BLUEPEARY JUICE

Ingredients
- 2 ripe pears
- 2 C spinach or baby spinach
- 1 c blueberries

79 MAGENTA ZINC

Ingredients
- Watermelon (¼ of a small size watermelon)
- Apples - 2
- Carrots - 4
- Beets - 1 with leaves
- Celery - 3 stalks
- Ginger - 1 inch

80 DARK KNIGHT

Ingredients
- Apples - 2
- Cucumber - 1
- Baby Celery - ½ bunch
- Carrots - 3
- Spinach - about ½ bunch
- Swiss Chard - 3 stalks

81 LEFTOVERS

Ingredients
- Strawberries - about 15
- Pineapples - 3 spears
- Watermelon - very little
- Celery - 3 stalks
- Cucumber - ¼
- Carrots - 2
- Dino Kale - 3 leaves
- Spinach - about ½ bunch

82 CITRUS SENSATION

Ingredients
- Pineapple - 2 spears
- Oranges - 2 to 3
- Strawberries - basketful
- Lemon - 1
- Apples - 2

83 BRIGHT GREEN GOODNESS

Ingredients
- Spinach - ½ bunch
- Dino kale - 8 leaves
- Cucumber - ½
- Celery - 4 to 5
- Baby celery
- Pineapple core
- Ginger - ½ inch

84 DELICIOUS MINT REFRESHER

Ingredients
- Pineapples spears - 4
- Strawberries - 1 basketful
- Apple - 1
- Mint leaves - about 30

85 MANGO TANGO

Ingredients
- Pineapple - 2 spears
- Strawberries - 7
- Mango - 1
- Nectarine - 1
- Apple - 1
- Orange - 1

86 GREEN AND ORANGE POWER

Ingredients

- Spinach - ½ bunch
- Carrots - 6
- Golden beets - 1
- Apple - 1
- Lemon - 1
- Orange - 1

87 RED CARROT ENVY

Ingredients

- Red carrots - 3
- Oranges - 1
- Apple - 1
- Cucumber - ½
- Baby celery

88 KALE SURPRISE

Ingredients

- Nectarine - 1
- Oranges - 2
- Dino kale - 8 leaves
- Red carrots - 2
- Apple 1

89 MIRACLE CURE JUICE

Ingredients

- 2 large beets
- 4 long carrots
- 2 apples (of any kind)
- 6 stalks celery
- 2 limes
- 2 inches ginger

90 LIGHT AND LEMONY ALOE JUICE

Ingredients

- 1 Cucumber
- 1 Apple
- 1 Lemon
- 2 tbsp Aloe vera pulp

91 HEALTH ALOE JUICE

Ingredients

- 1 Cucumber
- 1 Apple
- 1 Lemon
- 2 tbsp Aloe vera pulp
- Method:
- 1. Blend the apple and the cucumber
- 2. Add the lemon juice
- 3. Cut open an aloe vera leaf and scoop out 2 tbsp of the pulp and add it to the mixture

92 EXOTIC ALOE VERA JUICE

Ingredients

- 1-2 cup Fresh pineapple
- 1 Carrot
- 1 Green apple
- 1 tbsp Aloe vera pulp
- A few tbsp of coconut milk is optional

93 FRESH & FRUITY JUNGLE JUICE

Ingredients
- 6 cups of ice cubes
- 1 96 oz container of Tropical Punch Kool-Aid
- ½ container Orange Kool-Aid Liquid
- 1 bag of your favorite frozen fruit mix

94 NO MORE SINUS

Ingredients
- 2 carrots
- 2 oranges
- 1 green apple
- a small piece of ginger (optional)

95 CANCER FIGHTING GREEN JUICE

Ingredients
- 1 cup broccoli
- 1 cup cucumber
- 2 cup romaine lettuce
- ½ cup cilantro
- ½ green apple *optional
- 1 lime

96 ORANGE. SPINACH AND MINT

Ingredients
- ½ bunch of spinach
- 2 large navel oranges
- 2 mint leaves

97 LIVER CLEANSE GRAPE JUICE

Ingredients
- Water - 4-8 ounces (boiled and cooled)
- Fresh lemon - 1
- Ginger root - 1 inch, thinly sliced
- Grape juice
- 8 oz or 1 cup
- Flaxseed oil (or extra virgin olive oil)- 1 tbsp (slightly increase the quantity every day)
- Garlic cloves - 1 (increase by 1 clove each day)
- Cumin powder - 3 to 4 pinches
- Fresh Mint - 3 to 4 leaves (optional)

98 LIVER DETOXIFICATION VEGETABLE JUICE

Ingredients
- Fresh cabbage - 125 g
- Fresh lemon - 1
- Celery - 25 g
- Fresh pear - 250 g
- Ginger root - 1 inch
- Filtered Water - 500 ml
- Fresh Mint - 4 to 5 leaves

99 BELLY BUSTER GREEN JUICE

Ingredients

- 3 medium apples
- 1 large cucumber
- 1 large lemon, including skin
- 1 lime, including skin
- 3 small mandarins, including skin
- 1 head romaine lettuce

100 REBOOT ESSENTIALS

Ingredients

- 1 apple (large or medium)
- 1 lemon
- 4 celery stalks
- 2 medium-large carrots
- 6-10 stems parsley
- 6-8 stems fresh mint

III. 25 Nut milk recipes

Directions:

1. Soak the nuts in filtered water for 6-8 hours and rinse thoroughly.
2. Blend the ingredients for the recipe you are making on high for 1 min.
3. If you prefer nut milk without tiny nut bits, use a straining cloth to push the milk through
4. Re-blend for 45 seconds to 1 min (also optional).

Tip: For best results, blend the nuts in liquid 1-2 cups at a time. This will help your blender completely blend all nut pieces.

❶ PLAIN ALMOND MILK

Ingredients

- 1 cup soaked almonds
- 3-4 cups filtered water
- Additional filtered water for soaking almonds
- A sweetener such as 1-2 tbsp honey, maple syrup, agave, dates (5 or so) stevia etc.
- Optional flavorants such as cinnamon, vanilla, or cocoa

❷ CASHEW MILK

Ingredients

- 1 cup soaked cashews
- 4 cups water (divided)
- 1 to 2 tbsps maple syrup or honey or agave nectar
- 2 teaspoons vanilla extract
- dash sea salt
- pinch cinnamon (optional)

❸ EASY HOMEMADE HORCHATA

Ingredients

- 1 cup soaked cashews
- 2/3 cup white rice, uncooked (medium or long-grain preferred)
- 2 ½ cups water (first blend)
- 3 cups water (second blend)
- one 3-inch cinnamon stick
- 2/3 cup granulated sugar, or to taste*
- ½ teaspoon vanilla extract

❹ CASHEW MILK LATTES

Ingredients

- 1 ½ cups hot cashew milk
- 1 cup brewed coffee (preferably strong coffee)
- 2-3 large Medjool dates, pitted and roughly chopped
- 1 teaspoon vanilla extract
- pinch of ground cinnamon (to top with)

⑤ RAW CACAO HAZELNUT MILK

Ingredients

- 1 cup soaked unsalted organic hazelnuts
- 4 cups filtered or purified water
- pinch of himalayan sea salt
- 2 tbsps local raw honey or other sweetener
- 1 vanilla bean
- 2 tbsps raw cacao powder

⑥ VANILLA CINNAMON ALMOND MILK

Ingredients

- 1 cup soaked almonds, soaked in water
- 3.5 cups filtered water
- 2-4 pitted Medjool dates*, to taste
- 1 whole vanilla bean, chopped (or ½-1 tsp vanilla extract)
- ¼ teaspoon cinnamon
- small pinch of fine grain sea salt, to enhance the flavour

⑦ TURMERIC ALMOND MILK

Ingredients

- 1 cup organic soaked unsalted almonds
- 4 cups filtered or purified water
- pinch of himalayan sea salt (optional)
- 1 tbsp local raw honey or other sweetener (optional)
- 1-2 tbsps turmeric powder (I find turmeric to have a mild flavor, so I go with 2 tbsps)

⑧ NUT MILK WITH CHOCOLATE HAZELNUT AND HONEY CINNAMON CASHEW

Ingredients

- 1 cup soaked almonds, cashews, or hazelnuts
- 1 tbsp chia seeds
- 2 cups cold filtered water
- 2 cups coconut water
- 1-2 tbsps raw honey or 4 pitted dates soaked in warm water for about 5 minutes
- 1 teaspoon vanilla extract or ½ vanilla bean scraped
- 1 pinch fleur de sel or fine sea salt
- Chocolate Hazelnut Variation: 2 tbsps of unsweetened cocoa powder
- Cinnamon Cashew Variation: 1 teaspoon of good quality ground cinnamon

⑨ HOMEMADE RAW VEGAN BRAZIL NUT MILK

Ingredients

- 1 cup soaked brazil nuts
- 4 cups filtered water
- 4 pitted dates
- 1 pinch sea salt
- 1 tsp vanilla extract

⑩ PISTACHIO MILK

Ingredients
- 1 cup soaked unsalted organic pistachios
- 4 cups filtered or purified water
- pinch of himalayan sea salt
- 1 tbsp local raw honey or other sweetener
- 1 vanilla bean or 1 teaspoon vanilla extract (optional)

⑪ HOMEMADE PECAN MILK

Ingredients
- 1 cup soaked pecans
- 1 tsp vanilla extract
- 2 pitted dates OR 2 tbsp honey, agave, or maple syrup OR a dropper of liquid stevia (optional) tiny pinch of sea salt (the salt actually brings out the sweetness!)
- 5 cups water

⑫ STRAWBERRY MACADAMIA NUT MILK

Ingredients
- 1 cup soaked macadamia nuts (or almonds, or brazil nuts)
- 4 cups filtered water
- 2-3 cups sliced fresh strawberries
- 4-6 Pitted medjool dates
- 1 tbsp raw honey or maple syrup
- 1 teaspoon vanilla extract
- Pinch of sea salt

⑬ CASHEW CREAM

Ingredients
- 1 cup soaked cashews or macadamia nuts (120g)
- 1/3 cup to 3/4 cup water

⑭ GREEN CASHEW NUT MILK

Ingredients
- 1 cup of soaked cashews
- 4 cups of filtered water
- 10-12 dates
- 1 vanilla bean
- ¼ tsp sea salt
- 4 cups of spinach
- 4 cups of kale

⑮ VANILLA BEAN CASHEW MILK

Ingredients
- 1 cup soaked unsalted organic cashews
- 4 cups filtered or purified water
- pinch of himalayan sea salt
- 1 tbsp local raw honey or other sweetener
- 1 vanilla bean

⑯ HOMEMADE MACADAMIA NUT MILK

Ingredients
- ½ cup organic, soaked macadamia nuts
- 3½ cups cold water
- 4 Medjool dates, pitted
- ½ teaspoon vanilla extract

⓱ DECADENT ALMOND MACADAMIA MILK

Ingredients

- 50g macadamia
- 150g almond
- 30g dates
- 1 l of water

⓲ HOMEMADE ALMOND MACADAMIA ICED COFFEE

Ingredients

- ½ cup blanched almonds
- ¼ cup soaked macadamia nuts
- 6 pitted dates
- 2½ cups water

⓳ WALNUT COCONUT MILK WITH TURMERIC AND CINNAMON

Ingredients

- 1 cup soaked walnuts.
- 1 cup shredded coconut
- 1 tsp. Vanilla Extract
- 1 tsp. Cinnamon
- 1 tsp. Turmeric
- 1 tsp. Honey
- a pinch of pink Himalayan salt
- 4 cups of water

⓴ BANANA ALMOND AND OAT SMOOTHIE - ZUPAS

Ingredients

- 1 cup almond milk
- 1 tbsp natural peanut butter
- ¼ cup soaked whole almonds
- ¼ cup ground flax seed
- 1 cup plain Greek yogurt
- 1 tbsp honey
- ½ cup raw old fashioned oatmeal
- 2-3 bananas (best if cut into chunks and frozen)
- 1 tsp vanilla
- 1-2 dried dates (optional, to help sweeten)
- 2 cups crushed ice

㉑ PUMPKIN SPICE ALMOND MILK

Ingredients

- 1 cup soaked organic almonds (soaked overnight)
- 2 teaspoons vanilla extract or 1 vanilla bean (soaked with the almonds)
- 4 cups filtered water
- ½ cup organic pumpkin purée (canned or fresh)
- 2 teaspoons ground cinnamon
- ¼ teaspoon ground nutmeg
- pinch of ground ginger
- pinch of ground cloves
- 2 tbsps honey or maple syrup or a couple of soft medjool dates*
- pinch of sea salt

22 VANILLA WALNUT MILK

Ingredients

- 5 cups water
- 1 cup soaked walnuts
- 1 tbsps agave nectar
- 1 tbsp vanilla extract
- ¼ teaspoon sea salt

23 CHESTNUT PRALINE LATTE

Ingredients

- 1 cup (8 ounces) hot strong coffee
- ½ cup unsweetened cashew milk or other non-dairy milk, heated
- 3 roasted chestnuts (~ 1½ tablespoons)
- 6 toasted pecans (~ 1½ tablespoons)
- 2 tablespoons organic coconut sugar
- ½ teaspoon vanilla extract

24 ICED ALMOND-MACADAMIA MILK LATTE

Ingredients

- 1 generous cup/150 grams blanched almonds
- ½ cup/50 grams macadamia nuts
- 1/3 cup/40 grams pitted dates
- 1 liter filtered water

25 ORANGE SPLASH PISTACHIO MILK

- ½ cup soaked unsalted pistachio nuts
- 2 Tablespoons honey
- ¼ teaspoon ground vanilla or ½ teaspoon vanilla extract
- ⅛ teaspoon ground cardamom
- 2 pinches sea salt
- 1 teaspoon orange blossom water, more to taste

IV. 10 Nut butter recipes

> **Directions:**
> 1. Blend the nuts into a flour-like consistency first.
> 2. Add in rest of the ingredients according to the recipe.
> 3. Blend for 30-60 seconds.

❶ HOMEMADE ALMOND BUTTER

Ingredients
- 3 cups raw unsalted almonds
- 2 tbsps of coconut oil
- dash of sea salt
- Optional add ins:
- 1 tbsp of honey
- 1 tbsp of cinnamon

❷ PECAN BUTTER

Ingredients
- 8 ounces (about two cups) high quality pecans, either whole or in pieces
- sea salt, to taste
- dash of cinnamon

❸ WALNUT BUTTER

Ingredients

- 2 cups walnuts, shelled
- ¼ teaspoon salt
- 1 teaspoon honey
- 1 teaspoon roasted cinnamon
- 2 teaspoons walnut oil or grapeseed or canola oil

❹ CHOCOLATE HAZELNUT BUTTER SPREAD

Ingredients

- 18 ounces hazelnuts
- 3 tbsp – ¼ cup cocoa powder
- ¼ – ½ cup coconut sugar or granulated sugar
- ⅛ teaspoon salt

❺ CASHEW BUTTER

Ingredients

- 2 cups roasted cashews
- 2 tbsps organic coconut oil
- 1 tbsp pure vanilla extract
- ½ teaspoon sea salt

❻ PISTACHIO BUTTER

Ingredients

- 2 cups roasted pistachios
- ¼ tsp kosher salt
- 1 tbsp honey
- 1/8 tsp cinnamon

❼ PINE NUT BUTTER

Ingredients

- 2 cups of pine nuts
- 1 tbsp canola oil
- ¼ teaspoon fine grain sea salt

❽ MACADAMIA NUT BUTTER

Ingredients

- 1 pound macadamia nuts*
- 6 tbsps coconut oil
- pinch of salt
- 4-6 tbsps raw honey (optional)

❾ BRAZIL NUT BUTTER

Ingredients

- 2 cups organic raw brazil nuts
OPTIONAL ADDITIONS
- Salt
- Stevia, honey or maple syrup
- Vanilla or almond extract
- Raw cocoa powder or cacao nibs
- Puree of dried fruit

❿ HOMEMADE VANILLA CASHEW BUTTER

Ingredients

- 2 cups roasted cashews
- 2 tbsps organic coconut or vegetable oil
- 1 tbsp pure vanilla extract
- ½ teaspoon sea salt

V. 25 Easy Soup recipes

Directions:
1. Add all the ingredients you wish to liquify to make the soup (liquids first, then soft ingredients)
2. Turn on machine and increase speed over time to high (until heavy steam escapes vented lid)
3. Remove lid and add ingredients to add more textures to liquid soup (tomato chunks, croutons, veggies, etc.)
4. Re-blend for 1-5 seconds.

❶ MINESTRONE SOUP

Ingredients

- 1 (15 oz) can white beans, drained and rinsed
- 32 oz container reduced sodium chicken broth (or vegetable broth)
- 2 tsp olive oil
- ½ cup chopped onion
- 1 cup diced carrots
- ½ cup diced celery
- 2 garlic cloves, minced
- 1 (28 oz) can petite diced tomatoes
- Parmesan cheese rind (optional)
- 1 fresh rosemary sprig
- 2 bay leaves
- 2 tbsp chopped fresh basil
- ¼ cup chopped fresh Italian parsley
- ½ tsp kosher salt and fresh black pepper
- 1 medium 8 oz zucchini, diced
- 2 cups chopped fresh (or frozen defrosted) spinach
- 2 cups cooked small pasta such as ditalini or elbows (al dente)
- extra parmesan cheese for garnish (optional)

❷ TURKEY MEATBALL SPINACH TORTELLINI SOUP

Ingredients

- For the Meatballs:
- 10 oz 93% ground turkey
- 2 tbsp seasoned whole wheat breadcrumbs
- 2 tbsp grated parmesan cheese (Parmigiano Reggiano)
- 2 tbsp parsley, finely chopped
- 1 large egg
- 1 clove garlic, minced
- 1/8 tsp kosher salt

For the soup:
- ½ tbsp unsalted butter
- 2 stalks of celery, chopped
- 1 small onion, chopped
- 1 large carrot, peeled & chopped
- 2 cloves of garlic, minced
- 4 (14.5 oz) cans reduced sodium chicken broth
- 1 small Parmigiano-Reggiano rind (optional)
- 9 oz refrigerated spinach cheese tortellini
- fresh ground black pepper, to taste
- 3 cups loosely packed baby spinach
- fresh grated Parmigiano-Reggiano for topping

❸ HEARTY VEGETABLE SOUP

Ingredients

- 1 tbsp olive oil
- 1 teaspoon minced garlic
- 1 ½ pound lean ground beef
- ½ cup chopped onion
- 2 small potatoes, peeled and diced
- 1 cup chopped celery
- 1 cup chopped carrots
- 1 (14.5 ounce) can rotel
- 1 (15 ounce) can tomato sauce
- 1 cup water
- 1 tbsp balsamic vinegar
- 2 teaspoons chili powder
- ½ teaspoon kosher salt
- ½ teaspoon ground black pepper
- 3 tomatoes, diced

❹ CREAMY POTATO SOUP

Ingredients

- 30 oz. grated hash-brown potatoes
- 2 (14 oz.) cans chicken broth
- 1 (10.75 oz.) can cream of chicken soup
- ½ cup chopped onion
- ¼ teaspoon ground black pepper (more to taste)
- 1 (8oz) package cream cheese (softened)
- Optional Toppings: cheese, bacon, sliced green onions

❺ COPYCAT PANERA CREAMY TOMATO BASIL SOUP

Ingredients

- 1 28 oz can crushed tomatoes
- 1 28 oz can diced tomatoes
- 1 tbsp crushed garlic
- 1 14 oz can chicken broth {or 2 cups}
- 2 tbsp sugar
- 1/3 cup butter
- 1 cup heavy cream
- 15-20 basil leaves, chopped

❻ 5 - INGREDIENT BROCCOLI CHEESE SOUP

Ingredients

- 4 cups chicken stock
- 2 cups cooked broccoli florets, chopped
- ½ small onion, diced
- 15 oz can evaporated milk
- 2 cups shredded sharp cheddar cheese
- Salt and Pepper To Taste

❼ 8 CAN TACO SOUP

Ingredients

- 1 (15 oz.) can black beans, drained and rinsed
- 1 (15 oz.) can pinto beans, drained and rinsed
- 1 (14.5 oz.) can petite diced tomatoes, drained
- 1 (15.25 oz.) can sweet corn, drained
- 1 (12.5 oz.) can white chicken breast, drained
- 1 (10.75 oz.) can cream of chicken soup
- 1 (10 oz.) can green enchilada sauce
- 1 (14 oz.) can chicken broth
- 1 packet taco seasoning

❽ ROASTED CAULIFLOWER AND BROCCOLI WHITE CHEDDAR SOUP

Ingredients

- 1 large head cauliflower, cut into florets
- 1 medium head broccoli, cut into florets
- 1 tablespoon olive oil
- 8 strips uncooked bacon
- 2 medium onions, chopped
- ½ head garlic, minced
- 8 cups chicken stock
- 1 cup heavy cream
- 8oz (about 2 cups) shredded white cheddar cheese
- 2 tablespoons fresh thyme leaves, roughly chopped
- salt & pepper to taste

❾ SAUSAGE. POTATO AND SPINACH SOUP

Ingredients

- 1 tbsp olive oil
- 1 pound spicy Italian sausage, casing removed
- 3 cloves garlic, minced
- 1 onion, diced
- ½ teaspoon dried oregano
- ½ teaspoon dried basil
- ½ teaspoon crushed red pepper flakes, optional
- Kosher salt and freshly ground black pepper, to taste
- 5 cups chicken broth
- 1 bay leaf
- 1 pound red potatoes, diced
- 3 cups baby spinach
- ¼ cup heavy cream

❿ BEST EVER MUSHROOM SOUP

Ingredients

- 1 large white onion, diced
- 1 package white button mushrooms (10 oz) sliced
- 1 package baby portobello mushrooms (10 oz) sliced
- 10 stalks fresh thyme, leaves removed
- 1 cup organic vegetable broth
- 1 tbs. tapioca flour
- 1 cup almond or cashew milk (unsweetened)
- 1 dried bay leaf
- ½ tbs. liquid aminos (GF) (or soy sauce)
- ½ tsp. salt
- freshly ground pepper

⑪ QUICK AND EASY TOMATO SOUP

Ingredients

- 3 tbsps olive oil
- 2 tbsps butter
- 1 large sweet onion, finely chopped
- 2 large cloves garlic, minced
- 2 tbsps all-purpose flour
- 2 teaspoons dried basil
- 2 teaspoons dried thyme
- 4 cups chicken broth
- 56 ounces canned crushed tomatoes
- 2 teaspoons sugar
- ½ teaspoon kosher salt
- ½ teaspoon ground black pepper
- optional garnish: chopped fresh basil, chives, or dill

⑫ CREAMY CHICKEN AND MUSHROOM SOUP

Ingredients

- 1 tbsp olive oil
- 8 ounces boneless, skinless chicken thighs, cut into 1-inch chunks
- Kosher salt and freshly ground black pepper
- 2 tbsps unsalted butter
- 3 cloves garlic, minced
- 8 ounces cremini mushrooms, thinly sliced
- 1 onion, diced
- 3 carrots, peeled and diced
- 2 stalks celery, diced
- ½ teaspoon dried thyme
- ¼ cup all-purpose flour
- 4 cups chicken stock
- 1 bay leaf
- ½ cup half and half, or more, as needed*
- 2 tbsps chopped fresh parsley leaves
- 1 sprig rosemary

⑬ EASY CHICKEN AND RICE SOUP

Ingredients

- 1 tbsp extra-virgin olive oil
- 1 medium onion, chopped
- 2 garlic cloves, minced
- 2 medium carrots, cut diagonally into ½-inch-thick slices
- 2 celery ribs, halved lengthwise, and cut into ½-inch-thick slices
- 4 fresh thyme sprigs
- 1 bay leaf
- 2 quarts chicken stock or broth (we use low sodium)
- 1 cup of water
- 1 cup long grain white rice
- 1 ½ cups shredded cooked chicken breasts
- Kosher salt and freshly ground black pepper

⑭ QUICK & EASY CHINESE NOODLE SOUP

Ingredients

- 4 cups/1 Litre chicken Stock
- 2 – 3 Green/Spring onions – finely sliced into rounds
- 1 tbsp Oyster Sauce
- 1 tbsp Light Soy Sauce
- 1 tbsp Dark Soy Sauce
- 4 oz/200g Dried Chinese noodles
- 4 Bok Choy/Pak choi leaves, sliced

⑮ OLIVE GARDEN'S HOMEMADE ZUPPA TOSCANA SOUP

Ingredients

- 5-7 slices of cooked bacon
- ½ lb hot Italian Sausage
- 5 medium russet potatoes, washed and thinly sliced
- 2 cups kale, chopped
- 1 cups heavy whipping cream
- 1 quart water
- 2 cans chicken broth
- ½ large onion, finely chopped
- 4 medium cloves of garlic, minced
- 2 teaspoon red pepper flakes
- salt and pepper
- grated Parmesan for sprinkling

⑯ EASY CHEESEBURGER SOUP

Ingredients

- 1 pound ground beef, cooked
- 1 cup diced carrots
- ½ cup diced celery
- ½ onion, diced
- 1 tbsp butter
- 2-3 large potatoes, peeled and diced
- 4 cups chicken broth
- 1 teaspoon dried parsley
- 1 cup velveeta cheese, cubed
- 1 cup milk
- salt and pepper to taste

⑰ MISO SOUP

Ingredients

- 1 quart vegetable or chicken stock
- 2 cups water
- 2 to 3 tbsps Miso paste
- 1/3 of a 14 oz block of firm tofu, cut in small cubes
- 2 cups assorted mushrooms, sliced or left whole if very small
- 4 or 5 scallions, sliced thin (use all of the white and a little of the green)

18 BEST BUTTERNUT SQUASH SOUP

Ingredients

- 2 large roasted butternut squashes
- 1 pint of half and half
- ¾ stick of butter (browned)
- 2 tbsp of oil
- Salt and pepper to taste
- 2½ cups of chicken stock
- Creme fraiche to garnish

19 MEXICAN LIME SOUP W/ CHICKEN

Ingredients

- 3 or 4 limes
- 3 bone-in, chicken breast halves
- 1 tsp salt
- ½ tsp ground pepper
- 1 Tbs olive oil
- 1 large white onion, chopped
- 5 garlic cloves, minced
- 8 oz diced green chilies
- 4 cups low-sodium chicken broth
- 4 cups water
- 1 ½ tsp. ground cumin
- 1 avocado, peeled (sliced or chopped)
- Shredded Monterrey jack cheese

20 CREAMY SWEET POTATO SOUP

Ingredients

- 2 tbsps olive oil
- 1 small onion, diced
- 1 shallot, diced
- 2 cloves garlic, chopped
- 3-4 medium sized sweet potatoes (about 2 pounds), peeled cut into 1-inch cubes
- 4 cups chicken (or vegetable) stock
- ½ teaspoon cinnamon
- 1 teaspoon paprika
- 1 -2 teaspoons salt
- Fresh ground pepper

21 EASY CHICKEN NOODLE SOUP

Ingredients

- 4 cups water
- 1 can (14-½ ounces) chicken broth
- 1-½ cups cubed cooked chicken breast
- 1 can (10-3/4 ounces) condensed cream of chicken soup, undiluted
- 3/4 cup sliced celery
- 3/4 cup sliced carrots
- 1 small onion, chopped
- 1-½ teaspoons dried parsley flakes
- 1 teaspoon reduced-sodium chicken bouillon granules
- ¼ teaspoon pepper
- 3 cups uncooked egg noodles

㉒ CHICKEN ENCHILADA SOUP

Ingredients

1st Blend:
- 3 Roma or other small tomatoes
- 1 carrot
- 3 to 4 sweet peppers
- 1 celery stalk
- ½ cup mushrooms
- 4 sprigs cilantro
- 1 tablespoon taco seasoning
- 1 tablespoon tomato bouillon**
- ½ teaspoon garlic salt
- 3 cups water*

2nd Blend:
- 1 cup black beans (drained)
- 1 cup corn (drained)
- 1 cup cooked chicken, shredded or cubed
- 1 cup tortilla chips

㉓ ROASTED RED PEPPER SOUP

Ingredients
- 6-8 red bell peppers
- ½ an onion chopped
- 2 tbsps olive oil
- 5 cloves of garlic
- 4 cups of chicken stock
- 2 teaspoons hot sauce
- ½ teaspoon salt
- ½ teaspoon pepper
- ¼ cup sour cream
- 1 teaspoon dried oregano

㉔ 5-INGREDIENT EASY WHITE CHICKEN CHILI

Ingredients
- 6 cups chicken broth
- 4 cups cooked shredded chicken
- 2 (15-oz) cans beans, drained
- 2 cups salsa verde (store-bought or homemade)
- 2 tsp. ground cumin
- optional toppings: diced avocado, chopped fresh cilantro, shredded cheese, chopped green onions, sour cream, crumbled tortilla chips

㉕ CHICKEN QUINOA SOUP

Ingredients
- 2 tbsps olive oil
- 1 sweet onion, diced
- 2 large carrots, sliced diagonally
- 2 celery ribs, cut in half lengthwise
- 2-3 garlic cloves, minced
- 1 bay leaf
- 1 ½ teaspoons dried thyme
- 8 cups chicken broth
- 2/3 cups cooked quinoa
- 1 ½ cups shredded chicken
- salt and pepper

VI. 25 Fresh Spice blends

Directions:
1. Add desired herbs and raw spices according to recipe
2. Blend for 10-30 seconds on medium setting.

❶ BARBECUE CIRCUIT RUB

Ingredients
- Spice blend
- 3 tbsps cornstarch
- 2 tbsps chili powder
- 1 tbsp kosher salt
- 1 tbsp paprika (for more kick, use hot paprika)
- 1 teaspoon onion powder
- 1 teaspoon garlic powder
- 1 teaspoon sugar
- ½ teaspoon cumin
- ½ teaspoon cayenne pepper

Marinade
- 2 tbsps oil
- juice from one lime
- 2 tbsps spice blend
- 2 pounds of New York strip steak (skirt steak or sirloin work well too)
- 2-3 colored peppers
- 1 medium onion
- 1 tbsp oil
- 12 flour tortillas

❷ CAJUN SPICE MIX

Ingredients
- 1 teaspoon coarse salt
- 1 teaspoon ground black pepper
- 1 teaspoon onion powder
- 1 teaspoon cayenne pepper
- 1 teaspoon dried oregano
- 1 teaspoon dried thyme
- 2 teaspoons paprika
- 2 teaspoons garlic powder

❸ CHILI AND TACO SEASONING

Ingredients
- 4 tbsps of chili powder
- 1 teaspoon garlic powder
- 1 teaspoon onion powder
- 1 teaspoon crushed red pepper flakes
- ¼ teaspoon cayenne pepper
- 1 teaspoon dried oregano
- 2 teaspoons paprika
- 2 tbsps ground cumin
- 3 teaspoons sea salt
- 4 teaspoons black pepper

❹ CREOLE SEASONING BLEND

Ingredients

- ½ teaspoons black pepper, freshly ground
- ½ teaspoons white pepper
- ⅔ teaspoons cayenne pepper
- 1 teaspoon salt
- 2 teaspoons garlic powder
- 2 teaspoons onion powder
- 2 teaspoons oregano
- 2 teaspoons paprika
- 1 teaspoon thyme
- 1 teaspoon basil

❺ GREEK SEASONING

Ingredients

- 3 tbsps sweet paprika-
- ½ teaspoon Sea salt-
- ½ teaspoon Chopped onion
- ½ teaspoon Coriander seed
- ½ teaspoon Garlic salt
- ½ teaspoon Black peppercorns
- ½ teaspoon Turmeric
- ¼ teaspoon Minced garlic
- ¼ teaspoon Crushed red pepper
- ¼ teaspoon Dark chili powder
- ¼ teaspoon Mediterranean oregano
- ¼ teaspoon Sage

❻ GREEK SEASONING FOR CHICKEN GYROS

Ingredients

- 2 teaspoons salt
- 2 teaspoons dried oregano
- 1 ½ teaspoons onion powder
- 2 teaspoons garlic powder
- 1 teaspoon cornstarch
- 1 teaspoon pepper
- 1 teaspoon dried parsley flakes
- ½ teaspoon ground cinnamon
- ½ teaspoon grated nutmeg

❼ MONTREAL STEAK SEASONING

Ingredients

- 4 tbsps salt
- 1 tbsp black peppercorns
- 1 tbsp dehydrated onion
- ½ tbsp dehydrated garlic
- ½ tbsp crushed red pepper flakes
- 1 tbsp dried thyme leaves
- 1 tbsp dried rosemary leaves
- 2 teaspoons fennel seed

❽ OLD BAY SEASONING

Ingredients

- 1 tbsp paprika
- 1 tbsp ground bay leaves
- ½ tbsp celery salt
- 1 tsp black pepper
- ½ tsp red pepper flakes
- ½ tsp white pepper
- ½ tsp all-spice

9 PICKLING SPICE RECIPE

Ingredients

- 6 tbsp Mustard Seed
- 3 tbsp Whole Allspice
- 6 tsp coriander seed
- 6 whole cloves
- 3 tsp ground ginger
- 3 tsp red pepper flakes
- 3 bay leaves
- 3 cinnamon sticks

10 STEAK FAJITA SPICE BLEND

Ingredients

- 3 tbsps cornstarch
- 2 tbsps chili powder
- 1 tbsp kosher salt
- 1 tbsp paprika
- 1 teaspoon onion powder
- 1 teaspoon garlic powder
- 1 teaspoon sugar
- ½ teaspoon cumin
- ½ teaspoon cayenne pepper
- Marinade
- 2 tbsps oil
- juice from one lime
- 2 tbsps spice blend
- 2 pounds of New York strip steak
- 2-3 colored peppers
- 1 medium onion
- 1 tbsp oil
- 12 flour tortillas

11 POULTRY SEASONING

Ingredients

- 1 tbsp. rosemary
- 1 tbsp. oregano
- 2 tsp. sage
- 1 tbsp. ginger
- 1 tbsp. marjoram
- 1 tbsp. thyme
- 1 tsp. freshly ground black pepper

12 SPICY SWEET POTATO FRIES SPICE MIX

Ingredients

- 2 tbsp ground coriander
- 1 tbsp ground fennel
- 1 tbsp dried oregano
- 1 tbsp Aleppo Pepper
- 2 tbsp kosher salt

13 TACO SEASONING

Ingredients

- 2 TBSP Cumin
- 5 TBSP, 1 TSP Chili Powder
- 2 TSP Red Pepper Flakes
- 2 TSP Garlic Powder
- 2 TSP Onion Powder
- 1 TBSP, 1 TSP Paprika
- 2 TBSP, 2 TSP kosher salt
- 1 TBSP, 1 TSP black pepper

14 ZIPPY LEMON PEPPER RUB

Ingredients

- ½ teaspoons Black Pepper, Freshly Ground
- ½ teaspoons White Pepper
- ⅔ teaspoons Cayenne Pepper
- 1 teaspoon Salt
- 2 teaspoons Garlic Powder
- 2 teaspoons Onion Powder
- 2 teaspoons Oregano
- 2 teaspoons Paprika
- 1 teaspoon Thyme
- 1 teaspoon Basil

15 BASIC CURRY POWDER

Ingredients

- 2 dried red chiles, stemmed
- 1 tbsp coriander seeds
- 1 tbsp fennel seeds
- 1 teaspoon cumin seeds
- 1 teaspoon ground mace
- 1 teaspoon ground white pepper
- ½ teaspoon turmeric

16 CHINESE 5 SPICE BLEND

Ingredients

- 2 tbsps black peppercorns
- 2 tbsps whole cloves
- 3 cinnamon sticks, about 2-inches long
- 2 tbsps fennel seed
- 10 whole star anise

17 EGYPTIAN DUKKAH

Ingredients

- 1 cup nuts
- ½ cup sesame seeds
- ½ cup coriander seeds
- ¼ cup cumin seeds
- 1 teaspoon sea salt
- Freshly ground black pepper

18 ADOBO SEASONING

Ingredients

- 6 tbsps table salt
- 6 tbsps garlic powder
- 3 tbsps onion powder
- 3 tbsps ground black pepper
- 3 tbsps dried crushed Mexican oregano
- 3 tbsps ground cumin
- 3 tbsps anchiote seed seasoning
- 1-½ tbsps ground ancho chili powder
- 1-½ tbsps smoked paprika
- 1-½ tbsps ground turmeric
- 1-½ tbsps ground coriander

19 GARAM MASALA

Ingredients

- 1 heaping teaspoon whole cloves
- 1 ½ teaspoon black cardamom seeds (about 10 whole pods)
- 6 heaping tbsps cumin seed
- 1 tbsp pounded cinnamon sticks
- ¼ teaspoon ground mace
- ¼ teaspoon ground nutmeg

20 ETHIOPIAN BERBERE

Ingredients

- 1 teaspoon ginger
- ¼ teaspoon cinnamon
- ½ teaspoon cardamom
- ¼ teaspoon allspice
- ½ teaspoon coriander
- ½ teaspoon cumin
- ½ teaspoon fenugreek
- ½ teaspoon nutmeg
- ¼ teaspoon cloves
- 2 tbsps salt
- ¼ cup paprika
- ½ cup cayenne pepper

21 APPLE PIE SPICE BLEND

Ingredients

- ¼ cup ground cinnamon
- 2 teaspoons ground nutmeg
- 1 teaspoon ground allspice
- 1 teaspoon ground ginger

22 CHAI SPICE BLEND

Ingredients

- 2-4 cardamom pods (seeds only)
- 6-7 cloves
- 1 stick cassia cinnamon (1 cm x 4 cm in area), broken into tiny pieces
- 8-10 black peppercorns (smashed)
- 1 tbsp dried ginger powder

23 GINGERBREAD SPICE MIX

Ingredients

- 1 ½ teaspoons coriander seed
- 9 blades mace
- 15 cardamom pods
- 6 star anise petals
- 24 allspice berries
- 1 ½ teaspoons black peppercorns
- 6 teaspoons freshly ground ginger
- 1 ½ teaspoons ground cloves
- 1 ½ teaspoons ground cinnamon
- 3/4 teaspoon freshly grated nutmeg

24 YELLOW CURRY POWDER

Ingredients

- 2 tbsp whole coriander seeds
- 1 tbsp whole cumin seeds
- 2 tsp whole black peppercorns
- 1 ½ tsp whole brown mustard seeds
- 1 ½ tsp ground turmeric
- 1 tsp whole fenugreek seeds
- 3 hot dried red chilies, crumbled
- 3 whole cloves

25 ZA'ATAR SEASONING BLEND

Ingredients

- 2 tbsps dried thyme
- 2 tbsps dried sumac
- 2 tbsps sesame seeds, toasted or untoasted

VII. 25 Flavored coffee & tea blends

Directions:
1. When making hot drinks, use the more heat-resistant larger containers (40-64 oz)
2. Add the dry ingredients with some warm liquid and blend for 10-30 seconds to reduce to powder.
3. Next, add more liquid as necessary and blend until desired consistency is reached.

❶ SKINNY VANILLA FRAPPUCCINO

Ingredients
- 1 pkg. Starbucks Via (Breakfast Blend)
- 2 tbsp. sugar-free vanilla flavored coffee creamer, powdered
- ½ cup fat free milk
- 8-10 ice cubes
- 1 packet Truvia

❷ CHAI TEA FAUXCCINO

Ingredients
- 12 chai tea ice cubes (see notes above)
- 2 cups milks of choice (raw, almond or coconut)
- 2 tbsp maple syrup or raw honey (optional)
- whipped cream (optional)
- chocolate syrup (optional)
- salted caramel sauce (optional)

❸ PEPPERMINT MOCHA FRAPPE

Ingredients
- 4 oz Coffee-mate peppermint mocha creamer
- 2 tbsp mocha cappuccino mix
- 3 cups ice cubes
- whipped cream (optional)
- sugar/chocolate sprinkles for topping

❹ STRAWBERRY LEMONADE HERBAL TEA

Ingredients
- apple pieces,
- rosehip peels,
- apple slices,
- strawberry slices,
- strawberry pieces,
- natural and artificial flavoring,
- marigold petals,
- citric acid

❺ YOUTHBERRY WILD ORANGE BLOSSOM TEA BLEND

Ingredients

- apple pieces,
- white tea,
- hibiscus flowers,
- rose hip peels,
- apple slices,
- candied pineapple pieces
- candied mango pieces
- beetroot pieces,
- citrus slices,
- citrus peels,
- red currants,
- orange juice pieces,
- orange petals,
- rose petals,
- açai fruit powder

❻ CHOCOLATE CHIP COOKIE COFFEE CREAMER

Ingredients

- 1 can (14oz) sweetened condensed milk
- 1 ½ cup milk
- 3 tbsp unsweetened cocoa powder
- 3 tbsp light brown sugar, packed
- 2 tsp vanilla extract

❼ SKINNY ICE BLENDED MOCHA

Ingredients

- about 1½ cups crushed ice
- ½ cup non-fat milk
- ⅓ cup mashed ripe bananas
- 1 teaspoon pure vanilla extract
- 1 tbsp cocoa powder
- 2 teaspoons instant espresso powder
- 2 teaspoons granulated sugar

❽ CHOCOLATE FUDGE SUNDAE ICED COFFEE

Ingredients

- Donut Shop regular iced coffee K-cup
- 2 scoops vanilla ice cream
- hot fudge sauce, slightly warmed
- ice
- whipped cream

❾ GREEN TEA FRAPPE

Ingredients

- 1 cup non-fat milk
- 55 grams (about ½ cup) honeydew melon
- ¼ tsp. green tea powder
- ½ tsp. stevia
- ¼ tsp. vanilla extract
- 6 - 8 ice cubes
- ⅛ tsp. xanthan gum (optional)

⑩ LAVENDER TEA

Ingredients

- 3 cups of hot water
- 1 handful of fresh lemon balm. (Substitute mints or a couple of tea bags.)
- 2 tbsps fresh or dried lavender flowers.
- Honey to sweeten. (Optional.)

⑪ JACK FROST TEA

Ingredients

- ¼ cup dried peppermint leaves
- ¼ cup dried spearmint leaves
- 1 teaspoon of tisane
- 8 oz boiling water

⑫ MAKE YOUR OWN TRANQUIL TEA BLEND

Ingredients

- 4 parts chamomile
- 2 parts lemon grass
- 2 parts rose petals

⑬ NETTLE CINNAMON HERBAL TEA INFUSION

Ingredients

- 2 parts nettle
- 2 parts rose hips
- 1 part cinnamon chips
- 4 cups filtered water
- Ice (optional)
- Raw honey or fresh fruit juice (optional)

⑭ AFTER-DINNER DIGESTIVE TEA

Ingredients

- 3 ounces spearmint leaves
- 10.5 grams dried licorice root

⑮ APPLE GREEN TEA TURMERIC TONIC

Ingredients

- 4 parts nettle (Urtica dioica) leaf
- 3 parts spearmint (Mentha spicata) leaf
- 3 parts lemon balm (Melissa officinalis)
- 2 parts mullein (Verbascum thapsus) leaf
- 2 parts (combined) dandelion (Taraxacum officinale) leaf and root
- 2 parts red clover (Trifolium pratense) blossoms
- 1 part rose (Rosa spp.) hips
- 1 part Ginger Root (dried cut and sifted)

⑯ HOMEMADE BLACK APPLE TEA MIX

Ingredients

- 1 sweet organic apple
- 2 T lemon juice
- 2 t turbinado sugar
- ½ C loose leaf black tea
- 15 whole cloves
- 2 cinnamon sticks, broken (to break cinnamon sticks, place on towel and fold towel over. hit with heavy object several times)

⑰ ROSY BLACK TEA

Ingredients
- 2 parts rose petals
- 1 part black tea
- 8 oz boiling water

⑱ RUSSIAN TEA (NO POWDERED MIX)

Ingredients
- 4 cups water
- Juice of one lemon (approx ½ cup)
- Juice of two oranges (approx 1 cup)
- 2 tbsps honey
- 1 4" cinnamon stick
- 1 teaspoon whole cloves
- 4 black tea bags

⑲ SCHISANDRA FIVE-FLAVORED TEA

Ingredients
- 2 tbsp Schisandra berries
- 2 tbsp Elderberries (optional)
- 6 small pieces of licorice root, broken into small pieces
- 5-6 inch knob of ginger peeled and coarsely chopped
- A palmful or two of dried eleuthero
- 1-2 tbsp of dried green stevia leaves
- 1-2 cinnamon sticks, crushed

⑳ VITAMIN C HERBAL INFUSION

Ingredients
- 4 tbsps rose hips
- 1 tbsp lemongrass
- 1 tbsp cinnamon chips
- 1 teaspoon hibiscus flowers
- 1 teaspoon fennel seed
- ½ teaspoon lemon peel
- 4 cups filtered water
- (optional)
- Ice
- Raw honey or fresh fruit juice

㉑ SKINNY MINT CHOCOLATE CHIP FRAPPUCINO

Ingredients
- ¾ c double-strength coffee, chilled
- ½ c skim milk
- 2 tbsp unsweetened cocoa powder
- 1/8 tsp peppermint extract
- 2 c ice cubes
- sweetener, to taste (such as Stevia, Swerve, Truvia, etc.)
- ½ tsp miniature chocolate chips or dark chocolate, chopped

22 COCONUT WATER ICED COFFEE

Ingredients

- 1 cup coconut water
- 1/3-½ cup coffee concentrate
  Optional: cream or coconut creme for stirring

23 FRENCH VANILLA COFFEE CREAMER

Ingredients

- 1 can (14oz) Fat free sweetened condensed milk
- 1 ½ cup fat free milk (skim)
- 2 tsp vanilla extract

24 LEMON BALM TEA

Ingredients

- 2 tbsps dried lemon balm
- 1 tbsp dried oatstraw
- 2 teaspoons dried, seedless rosehips
- 1 ½ teaspoons dried orange peel
- ½ teaspoon dried lavender

25 HOMEMADE CINNAMON COFFEE

Ingredients

- 10 cups of water
- 3 whole cinnamon sticks
- 3 heaping teaspoons brown sugar
- 1 cup ground coffee (unflavored)
- 1 teaspoon cinnamon

VIII. 20 Milkshake Recipes

Directions:
1. Add soft ingredients and mix with liquid as per recipe.
2. Blend until desired consistency is achieved. Add more liquid to make less thicker shakes.
3. Open lid and add toppings to introduce more textures (crunchy candy pieces,soft fruit,etc.)
4. Blend for 1-10 seconds if you want additional ingredients mixed in.

❶ CAKE BATTER MILKSHAKE

Ingredients
- 2 cups vanilla ice cream
- 1 cup milk
- ½ cup vanilla or funfetti dry cake mix
- Sprinkles (optional)

❷ FROZEN CARAMEL HOT CHOCOLATE

Ingredients
- 2 cups prepared caramel hot chocolate
- 2 cups ice
- ¼ cup Caramel ice cream topping
- 1 cup Non-fat Cool Whip
- ¼ cup Rolos, chopped in half (optional)
- ¼ cup caramel chips (optional)

❸ COOKIE MONSTER ICE CREAM

Ingredients
- 2 cup vanilla ice cream
- 14 oz sweetened condensed milk
- 1 tbsp vanilla extract (optional)
- ½ tsp blue food coloring
- 5 chocolate sandwich cookies (like Oreos)
- 2 chocolate chip cookies

❹ STRAWBERRY NUTELLA MILKSHAKE

Ingredients
- ½ cup milk
- ½ cup strawberries
- 2 big scoops of vanilla ice cream
- ¼ cup Nutella
- Whipped cream, sprinkles, and extra Nutella, optional for serving

⑤ KIT KAT MILKSHAKE

Ingredients

- 1 Kit Kat bar (broken)
- 2 cups vanilla ice cream (or frozen yogurt)
- ½ cup milk
- 1 teaspoon vanilla extract
- Hershey's chocolate syrup
- Whipped cream

⑥ MINI S'MORE BROWNIE

Ingredients

- 1 box brownie mix
- Mini graham cracker pie crusts
- Mini marshmallows
- Chocolate chips
- Crushed graham crackers

⑦ NERDS MILKSHAKE

Ingredients

1st Blend:

- 3 scoops vanilla ice cream (or 1 heaping cup)
- ½ cup milk

2nd Blend:

- one 1.65 ounce package strawberry & grape Nerds candy, extra if desired for garnish
- whipped cream for topping if desired

⑧ SUPER EASY NUTELLA MILKSHAKE

Ingredients

- 2 scoops of Vanilla ice cream
- 4 Tbsp of Nutella (be generous!)
- 2 cups of milk

⑨ STRAWBERRY MILKSHAKE

Ingredients

- 1 cup milk
- 1 teaspoon vanilla
- 1 pound strawberries (hulled)
- 2 cups vanilla ice cream

⑩ COTTON CANDY MILKSHAKE

Ingredients

- 3 scoops of vanilla ice cream
- 2 tablespoons of milk
- 4 ice cubes
- 6 big puffs of cotton candy

⑪ BANANA CREAM PIE MILKSHAKE

Ingredients

- 1 cup Plain, Nonfat Greek Yogurt
- ¼ cup Unsweetened Vanilla Almond Milk
- ¼ tsp Vanilla Flavored Stevia Extract
- 1 medium Banana, very ripe
- Crushed graham crackers

⑫ SNICKERS & PRETZEL MILKSHAKE

Ingredients

- 2 cups chocolate ice cream
- 4 fun-sized Snickers bars (or any chocolate bar of your choice)
- 1 package of pretzel sticks, broken up

⑬ MOCHA MINT MILKSHAKE

Ingredients

- 4 cups mint chocolate chip ice cream
- ½ cup chocolate syrup
- ½ cup cold strong coffee
- ½ cup milk
- ¼ cup chocolate syrup, for cup swirls
- ¼ cup chopped Andes mints
- Whipped cream, for garnish

⑭ RED VELVET MILKSHAKE

Ingredients

- 4 scoops red velvet ice cream
- 1 cup of milk
- 3-4 drops red food coloring (optional)
- whipped cream
- peppermint candies, crushed
- maraschino cherries

⑮ TOASTED MARSHMALLOW MILKSHAKE

Ingredients

- 5 scoops high-quality vanilla ice cream
- 2 tablespoons whole milk
- 1 tablespoon plain greek yogurt
- 5 jumbo toasted marshmallows (can toast in oven or over stove)
- Whipped cream, for topping
- Graham crackers, crushed, for garnish

⑯ COFFEE MILKSHAKE

Ingredients

- 1 cup cold-brewed coffee (see recipe below for instructions, or use strong brewed coffee that has been well chilled.)
- 4 giant scoops vanilla ice cream
- 1 tablespoon chocolate syrup plus extra for drizzling
- whipped cream

⑰ MANGO MILKSHAKE

Ingredients

- 1 cup - chopped mango
- 2.5 cups - chilled milk
- 2 tsp - sugar (or as needed)
- 1 - green cardamom (optional)
- ice cubes (optional)

⓲ MINT CHIP MILKSHAKE CUPCAKES

Ingredients

- 1 frozen, large banana
- ½ tsp pure vanilla extract
- 2 Tbsp melted coconut butter
- ½ to ⅔ cup milk of choice

⓳ CHOCOLATE COOKIE DOUGH MILKSHAKE

Ingredients

- 1 ¼ cups Chocolate Milk
- 5-6 scoops Cookie Dough Ice Cream
- Chocolate Syrup
- Whipped Cream
- Cherries (optional)

⓴ ULTIMATE ICE CREAM SUNDAE MILK

Ingredients

- 1 Serving of Chocolate Syrup or Fudge (approx 2 Tbs)
- 3 Large Fresh Strawberries
- 1 Medium Ripe Banana

- 1 Serving of Vanilla Ice Cream or Frozen Yogurt (softened)
- TruMoo Chocolate Milk

IX. 25 DIY Whipped Natural butters for Hair, Skin, and Body

Directions:
Body Butters & Creams:
1. Combine butter and oil ingredients in container and blend on medium until everything is blended smoothly.
2. Add incense drops and blend for 1-5 seconds.

❶ WHIPPED GINGERBREAD BODY BUTTER

Ingredients
- ½ cup Shea butter
- ¼ cup coconut oil
- 2 tbsp. almond oil
- 2 tsp or 2 Vitamin E capsules
- 2 tsp. Ground Ginger
- 1 tsp. Ground Cinnamon
- 1 tsp. Vanilla Extract

❷ SKIN PERFECTING BODY BUTTER

Ingredients
- 2oz shea butter
- 2oz evening primrose oil
- 10 drops Young Living Jasmine oil
- 10 drops Young Living Frankincense oil

❸ HOMEMADE BODY BUTTER WITH SHEA AND COCONUT OIL

Ingredients
- ½ cup shea butter
- ¼ cup coconut oil
- ¼ cup olive or almond oil
- 10-15 drops essential oil, orange, or sandalwood

❹ DREAMY HOMEMADE LEMON CREAM BODY BUTTER

Ingredients
- 6 tbsps coconut oil
- ¼ cup cacao butter
- 1 tbsp vitamin E oil
- ¼ teaspoon lemon essential oil

❺ MANGO BODY BUTTER

Ingredients
- 1 cup shea butter
- ½ cup mango butter
- ½ cup almond oil
- Mango essential oil (20-25 drops)

⑥ HOMEMADE BODY BUTTER BASE

Ingredients

- ½ cup each of organic
- cocoa butter
- shea butter
- coconut oil
- olive oil
- ½ teaspoon of essential oils

⑦ WHIPPED MOCHA BODY FROSTING

Ingredients

- 30g white cocoa butter
- 30g dark cocoa butter (or just more white cocoa butter)
- 60g shea butter or mango butter
- 40g olive oil (or other relatively plain liquid oil)
- 4 drops coffee essential oil

⑧ CRANBERRY BODY BUTTER

Ingredients

- 3 oz. refined shea butter
- .25 oz. refined/deodorized cocoa butter
- .2 oz. grape seed oil
- .1 oz. Cyclomethicone
- .05 oz. pure tapioca starch
- .1 oz. cranberry fragrance oil of choice
- pinch coral oil locking mica shimmer, optional

⑨ HONEY COCONUT BODY BUTTER

Ingredients

- 8g beeswax
- 36g virgin coconut oil
- 2 drops clove bud essential oil
- 25 drops labdanum essential oil

⑩ ECZEMA RELIEF BODY CREAM

Ingredients

- ¼ cup Shea butter
- ¼ cup coconut oil
- 10 drops Lavender essential oil
- 5-10 drops Cedarwood essential oil
- a few drops of vitamin E oil (optional)

⑪ WHIPPED SHEA BUTTER FOR HAIR & BODY

Ingredients

- 4 oz Raw shea butter, softened
- 6 tsp Virgin (unrefined) coconut oil, softened
- 4 tsp Castor oil
- 1 tsp Jojoba oil
- 8 tsp Aloe Vera Gel

⓬ BASIC BODY BUTTER

Ingredients

- 1-3/4 cups shea butter (unrefined is best)
- ½ cup coconut oil (extra virgin is best)
- ¼ cup grapeseed oil
- essential oils

⓭ COOLING ALOE AND MINT BODY LOTION

Ingredients

- ¼ cup grated beeswax
- ½ cup coconut oil
- ½ cup aloe vera gel, room temperature
- ⅛ teaspoon peppermint oil

⓮ PEPPERMINT BODY BUTTER

Ingredients

- 3 ounces pure cocoa butter
- 4 ounces coconut oil
- 4 drops peppermint essential oil
- 2 drops red food coloring

⓯ HOMEMADE BABY SKIN CREAM

Ingredients

- ¼ cup cocoa butter (or 32 cocoa butter wafers)
- ¼ cup shea butter
- 2 tbsps olive oil
- 1 tbsp castor oil

⓰ CHOCOLATE HAZELNUT BODY LOTION

Ingredients

- 14g cocoa butter
- 22g hazelnut oil
- 14g emulsimulse (or other complete emulsifying wax)
- 146 mL water
- 4g vegetable glycerin
- 1 blob/drop benzoin essential oil
- 2 drops cocoa absolute

⓱ WHIPPED WHITE CHOCOLATE BODY BUTTER

Ingredients

- ¼ cup shea butter
- ¼ cup cocoa butter
- ¼ cup coconut oil
- ¼ cup sweet almond oil
- 10-20 drops of essential oil

⓲ DOUBLE CHOCOLATE BODY BUTTER

Ingredients

- 1 cup cocoa butter (approximately 5 oz)
- ½ cup pure virgin coconut oil
- 1 tsp beeswax pastilles
- 2 tbsp almond oil
- 1 tbsp pure vanilla extract
- 1 ½ tbsp raw cacao powder

⑲ HOMEMADE NOURISHING FACE CREAM

Ingredients

- ½ cup coconut oil
- ½ cup shea butter
- ¼ cup of almond oil
- 5-6 drops of essential oil

⑳ HOMEMADE FACE LOTION

Ingredients

- 3 ½ tbsp organic Shea butter
- 2 tbsps Jojoba oil
- 3 tbsps of Aloe Leaf Juice
- 4 drops lavender essential oil of choice
- A pint sized mason jar
- a small glass jar

㉑ WHIPPED PEPPERMINT BARK BODY BUTTER

Ingredients

- ¼ cup cocoa butter
- ¼ cup shea butter
- ¼ cup coconut oil
- 2 Tbs. vitamin E oil
- ¼ tsp. peppermint extract

㉒ PRETTY IN PINK BODY BUTTER

Ingredients

- 1 cup coconut oil
- 1 ½ cup vegetable shortening
- 1-3 drops pink food dye
- 5-10 drops essential oils (optional)

㉓ BEACH BUTTER BALM

Ingredients

- 2 oz. Cocoa butter – Natural
- 2 oz. Shea butter – natural
- 2 oz. Monoi butter
- 1 tsp. Argan oil
- 3 tsp. Sweet almond oil
- 3 tsp. Aloe vera Gel
- ¼ tsp. Vitamin E Natural
- 9.5 mL(s) Exotic coconut fragrance oil

㉔ LEMON CREAM BODY BUTTER

Ingredients

- 6 tbsps coconut oil
- ¼ cup cacao butter
- 1 tbsp vitamin E oil
- ¼ teaspoon lemon essential oil

㉕ ULTRA HEALING FOOT CREAM

Ingredients

- ¼ cup olive oil infused with calendula and chamomile
- ¼ cup lavender infused coconut oil
- ¼ cup cocoa butter
- 25g grated beeswax
- 25 drops peppermint essential oil
- 10 drops lemongrass essential oil
- 5 drops vanilla essential oil
- 5 drops tea tree essential oil
- 5 drops lavender essential oil

It's a fact: readers who follow an ACTION GUIDE as they read and use cookbooks tend to have the most success!

Here's what I'm going to do to thank you for downloading my book. Go to the link below to instantly sign up for these bonuses.

Here's just a taste of what subscribers get:

Printable Kitchen Guides:

- Keep your food fresher for longer with the Extra-Long Food Storage Guide
- No more guess work in the kitchen -- Metric Conversion Guide
- Make delicious spreads in minutes -- Easy Spreads Guide
- Protect your family from consuming undercooked meat -- Meat Grilling Guide
- Many more new upcoming high-quality guides

Books and Recipes:

- New mouth-watering recipes you have NEVER tried before
- New books I publish for FREE

GRAB YOUR FREEBIES NOW AT
COOKINGWITHAFOODIE.COM

Made in the USA
Monee, IL
16 August 2023

41118674R00062